INTRODUCTION

Hero was a name given by the Greek poet H(omer?) to (men of?) strength, courage or ability, presumed to (be favoured?) by the gods. In later times heroes were believed to be intermediate between gods and men, and to be immortal. Until the twentieth century heroic qualities were generally believed to exist only in men. Modern usage tends towards using 'hero' to describe a particularly brave man or woman.

All of the folk mentioned here had a connection with Kingswear at some time in their lives. Their bravery, sacrifice or exceptional devotion to duty is acknowledged with deep gratitude. Some were praised and rewarded in their life-times, while others received little in the way of public acknowledgement. Two fictional stories have been included because they have been accepted by some people as having belonged to a real hero and a real heroine. Historians try not to become sentimentalists: we try to explain the truth behind these misunderstandings.

Some of our earlier heroes may seem to have surprising new biographies. It is the responsibility of historians or archaeologists to collect all of the known facts relating to the person or place under discussion. Where direct information is lacking comparisons with similar persons or places may shed some, probably correct, information. When all direct and background evidence is assembled, a first draft of history may be considered. A form of correctness demands that we should admit defeat and let the reconstructed story rest there. Not so with your current authors, we unashamedly maximize the possibilities in order to stimulate reassessment of all the evidence, and a spirited re-evaluation of previous interpretations. It should be our aim to promote research, through documents, landscape analysis, targeted excavations, and laboratory analysis of excavated artifacts and samples.

We do not compare one act of bravery with another: they are listed here in neutral alphabetical order. We must emphasize that these are the heroes and heroines that we have found so far in our attempt to systematically analyse all of the Kingswear records. There will have been others from earlier centuries whose names and deeds have not been recorded or remembered.

- Were men from our manors alongside King Harold at Stamford Bridge or Hastings?
- Were there Kingswear men at Agincourt with King Harry?
- Did any of our men crew for Drake or for Gilbert out of Greenway?
- How many fought for Parliament against demented King Charles?
- Who might have been at Blenheim, or at Trafalgar, or at Waterloo?

Other heroes will probably be rediscovered, and we will find ways by which their deeds can be added to this list. If any members of their families should read this tribute we would be very grateful if they were to introduce themselves or offer information or photos.

THE KINGSWEAR WAR MEMORIALS AND WAR GRAVES

The Kingswear War Memorial relating to the Great War of 1914-1918 is on the north wall of the nave of the Church of Saint Thomas of Canterbury, Kingswear. It is a wooden triptych inscribed "To the Glory of God and in grateful memory of the men of this parish who gave their lives in the Great War. Their names liveth for evermore."

William Bell
Frederick Charles Brewster
Valentine Francis Gibbs
Harry Hamlyn
William Vivian Jolliffe
Richard Giles Todd

Douglas Boyd-Carpenter
Richard Lawrence Luscombe Caunter
Charles Ernest Hamlyn
Harry Horseman
Charles Edward Ryder
William John Tolman

Added to the 1914-18 Memorial are the names of those that fell during World War II of 1939-1945

'Remember - Grant them O Lord eternal rest and let light perpetual shine upon them'

Russell Arthur Brown
John Seton Kyffin
Charles Frederick Knapman
Reginald Perring
Charles Earsham Turner
Frederick Howard Thompson

Alfred Evans
James Henry King
Herbert George Little
John Rutter
Arthur Toms

Also on the north wall is a wooden panel inscribed 'In memory of the men and women who lost their lives by enemy action at Noss Shipyard September 18th 1942'.

Frederick C. Adams
David Bott
Rose A. Crang
Richard Franklin
Walton Lewis
Henry J. Luckhurst
Sidney Pope
Hubert E. W. Putt
Nellie E. Trebilcock
Frederick Vickery

John R. Ash
John G. C. Bustin
Thomas Farr
Lionel E. Holden
George H. F. Little
John Martin
Ernest Poole
Edward E. Trant
Samuel J. Veale
Hazel J. Weaver

This monument was originally at the Noss works but on its closure was re-located in Kingswear church. So far we have not found any documents relating to the erection of these memorials, or relating to how the names were researched or chosen for inclusion. One name is a recent addition. It is a pity that the material used does not match the original woodwork. There are War Graves in Kingswear Cemetery, looked after by the Imperial War Graves Commission.

MAUD MARY ANN ASH
BRAVERY IN A FIRE

Maud Mary Ann Ash was born in Churston Ferrers in 1888. Her parents were James and Emma Cole. The 1891 census lists the family at Churston. The 1901 census lists her still at Churston with father James listed as Green Keeper at the Links. She married Charles Ash, a Dartmouth coal lumper, in 1906. A lumper was a casual labourer who moved coal (often by carrying it in baskets) from cargo steamers to hulks in the estuary and then on to steamers to fuel their boilers. On a few days his earnings might have been good, but taken over a year they would have been meagre. By March 1912 Maud was aged 23, and she was living with husband Charles, aged 26, in three rented rooms in Newcomen House, an old timber-framed Dartmouth building in Newcomen Road, Dartmouth.

It might have been the house once lived in by Thomas Newcomen when he invented his steam engine. They had not yet had any children. Maud's mother, Mrs. Mary Ann Cole, by now aged 61, lodged with them. The frontage of the house had been used for some years by Mr. Drake as a general dealer's shop with a store behind. The rest of the building was crudely divided into tenements which held 32 residents including Maud Ash's family. The gazetteer on the back page of the Dartmouth Chronicle, published on the Friday before the fire, ignores the house and its occupants. The owner of the house was Mr. R. Cary of London; his agent was Mr. W. Denning of Victoria Road, Dartmouth.

The occupants of the house went to bed as usual on Sunday night the 7th March 1912. At about half past midnight Frank Pound, a coal lumper, was on the Embankment and saw flames in Newcomen Road. He ran up the steps from Lower Street and raised the alarm. In the near silent midnight of 1912 his shouts of 'Fire' could be heard in the adjacent streets and police constable Stuart, patrolling his beat, ran to the scene. The fire had probably spread from a kitchen next to the store-room of the shop; lard and candles were in the store. The door of the store had been left open so that the cat could deal with the rats. The only access to the tenements from the street was by a narrow passage which was already filled with flames. Next to the burning property was a school playground.

Frank Pound was helped to climb over the gate, with its spiked railings on top, jumped into the playground and opened it from within. Charles Ash jumped from a window into this playground and was injured. It is not clear from the newspaper version of events that night why he had needed to do this. Onlookers and helpers took him to Dartmouth Cottage Hospital. He is not listed among the injured later to be mentioned in the Chronicle. Messengers were sent to the police station and to the fire station. The police sergeant and two more constables were soon on the scene. A telephone call was made to the Naval College asking for urgent assistance. The college sent more than forty men to help, including a party of marines with rifles. Perhaps a worldly-wise officer feared looting after the blaze. The fire brigade responded promptly by 1912 standards. The steam fire engine was put to use and a ladder was put to the windows on Newcomen Road. Renwick and Wilton's tug *Totnes* was moored on the embankment and its pumps also poured water on the fire.

Soon after midnight Maud was awakened by a shout of 'Charles Ash - Your house is on fire'. She roused her husband saying someone is shouting 'Fire'. The stairs to the street were already burning and Maud's kitchen was filled with smoke and heat. The tenements were divided by the doors of the old house which were bolted on both sides Maud knocked on a door between her rooms and those of a neighbour. After a time the neighbour unbolted her side of the door. Escape was now possible down another flight of stairs and she reached the safety of a garden or clothes-drying ground behind the house. This 'garden' soon filled with men, women and children, clad in their nightwear. Some were injured. It was raining. They were still in danger from falling slates, smoke and tar dripping from the tarred and felted roof. A policeman organised their removal to a safer place, further up the garden. The neighbouring properties had also to be evacuated. As soon as possible these unfortunate people were escorted to the homes of relatives or friends. Mr. and Mrs. Hayball (Gazetteer says 48 Newcomen Road) provided shelter that night for a number of people.

Maud knew that her mother was in a room beyond her kitchen and beyond the blazing stairs. She re-entered the building through the smoke and heat, avoiding falling slates, beams and brickwork, to find her mother unconscious on the floor of her room. Grasping her hair she lifted the 'old woman' out of the building to the garden where others revived her. The Callard family were still in the building. Herbert J. Callard had earlier appeared at a window holding his son Walter aged 9. He shouted 'Look out' and dropped his son, evidently hoping that someone would catch him. The lad struck the shoulders of Mr. Partridge and then fell heavily on the ground. He was taken to the Hospital with severe internal injuries.

Maud now knew that Mr. Callard and his wife and three other children were still in the burning building. She entered the building a second time with her nightdress now tied around her head. She found Callard and dragged him out before she collapsed. Callard was unconscious for half an hour. A policeman gave Maud his cape and arranged for someone to lend her a skirt. The policemen tried to reach Mrs. Callard and her children but were driven back by the flames and smoke. The police sergeant and members of the volunteer fire brigade were later to be highly praised for their efforts at fire control and their attempts to rescue Mrs. Callard and her children. The bodies were recovered from the collapsed ruins by the police and volunteers after the fire was extinguished. They were only identified by their sizes.

The various paragraphs of the Chronicle story give slightly conflicting versions of that confused and terrible night, so the stories of Maud Ash and her neighbour, George Adams, is quoted here as printed:-

Mrs. Maud Mary Ann Ash was interviewed soon after the fire. Her only sorrow appeared be that she had not succeeded in saving the lives of Maud Callard and her three children.

"I aroused my husband, got out of bed and opened the door of my bedroom. The room was immediately filled with smoke that was so thick that we could not see each other. I ran to the top of the stairs but found that our escape by that way was cut off as the stairs were blazing. I at once returned to my mother's bedroom and found mother overcome by the smoke. I dragged her out by the hair and carried her up the stairs to a fastened-up door leading to Mrs. Adam's rooms. Then I shouted 'Help!' and knocked at the door. Mrs. Adams opened the door and helped me through the passage with mother to the back garden. I then went back to Mr. Callard's room and I heard Mrs. Callard and her husband, but the smoke was so thick that I could not see them. I got hold of him and dragged him as far as the passage, when I was overcome by the smoke.

I had to let go in order to get out and obtain some fresh air, and I then tied my nightdress around my mouth and went back again. Owing to the smoke being so thick I could not see anyone, but I heard Mr. Callard shouting 'For God's sake, Maud, try and keep up'. His wife replied 'I can't Herb, I can't'. I heard someone fall with a crash. I was overcome by the smoke and had to go out again to get fresh air. I returned a third time. When I got to Mr. Adams' rooms I felt someone catch hold of my hair at the back and it proved to be Mr. Callard. I got hold of him and carried him as well as I could into the garden and laid him down. I fell over him because I was quite overcome. I know Mother and Mr. Callard were afterwards carried further up the garden. We had nothing on but our nightclothes. I told a policeman that Mrs. Callard and her children were still in the room. No person could live in that smoke very long."

Mr. George Adams, a fisherman, had lived in the house for thirty five years. He occupied the three top rooms." I heard someone crying 'Fire'. I smelt burning but there was no smoke then. I got out my wife and granddaughter. There was a fastened door between my rooms and those occupied by the Callards. I heard someone knocking at the door and a cry of 'Help, let us out'. I took away the things and opened the door when I was met by the smoke which was so black that I could not see anyone. I carried away a tin box.

Mrs. Ash was pushing her mother out of the passage. I helped them out to the garden acting as a guide. Mrs Ash ran back again. I did not know she was gone until I heard her screaming 'Won't somebody help me, I'm choking'. I went down the passage and met Mrs. Ash. She was carrying Callard. Her arms were round his body under the arm pits. I took hold of his legs and helped him out. I went out backwards. We got him in the garden. The smoke was too black to allow us to see each other. Callard was unconscious; I thought he was dead. The flames came up behind us and it was impossible to go in again although I tried."

The Dartmouth Chronicle listed the victims as:-
Maud Mary Ann Callard - 34 years, married - Dead.
Florence Honor Callard - 10 years - Dead.
Victor John Callard - 12 months - Dead.

Frederick Callard - 10 days - Dead.
Herbert J. Callard - Suffering from shock.
Walter Callard - 9 years - Abdominal injuries.
Mrs. Bulley - Fractured leg.
Mrs. Lidster - Injured.
Fireman Whitemore - Injured.
Fireman Evans - Injured.

With regard to Maud's modesty, we can deduce that poor folk living in an unheated house during March might well have slept in their underclothes beneath their nightdresses or nightshirts. Several people, including Maud, were overcome for a time by the smoke, but seem to have recovered quite quickly. The smoke from this fire came only from wood and other natural organic materials. It would not have contained the toxins derived from later twentieth century plastics.

The Mayor, the Coroner and the inquest jury all remarked on Maud's bravery. They seem to imply that such bravery might have been expected from a man but was exceptional in a woman. The inquest jury, after giving their verdict on the death of Mrs. Callard and her children as 'Misadventure', expressed their appreciation of the heroic deeds of Mrs. Ash, and hoped that some means could be found of obtaining suitable recognition for her bravery.

On the 30th of August 1912 there was a presentation by the Mayoress of Dartmouth (Mrs. C. Hampton), at the Guildhall, in the presence of many distinguished citizens, to Maud Ash of a framed illuminated certificate and a cheque for £5 awarded by the Society for the Protection of Life from Fire. The Mayor, Mr. C. Peek, gave great praise to all who been involved and had done their duty during that terrible night. He also said that he had intended saying something regarding the ungratefulness of Mr. Callard, but perhaps on this occasion it would be better not to enlarge upon it.

We should remember that in 1912 the effects of stress and shock were hardly recognised and certainly not understood. No counselling for grief, beyond kind words (whether with tact and wisdom or without) from other family members would have been available. To-day we have no other evidence with which to assess Herbert Callard's words or actions in reaction to his great loss.

On September 27th 1912 there was a further presentation by the Mayor, accompanied by other local dignitaries, to Maud Ash of a framed certificate and a cheque for £20 from the Carnegie Heroes Trust. The speeches made it clear that the Mayor and his colleagues had gone to great trouble to secure this award.

In April of this year the *Titanic* had sunk. Probably the Carnegie Heroes Trust had had many cases to consider. In the speeches much was made of the fact that this bravery was enacted by a woman. Maud was clearly very meek and humble in her acceptance of her awards and we might remember that at this time well-bred ladies were being imprisoned for being militant suffragettes. Apparently Maud had no inclination to use her fame for any political cause. The tragedy started a half-hearted debate in Dartmouth regarding slum clearance but no action was taken at this time.

In 1916 Maud and Charles had a son, probably their only child, George Charles Edward Ash.

From about 1935 onwards the Dartmouth and Kingswear Directory and other lists mention Mr and Mrs Charles Ash as living at Railway View, 1 Church Hill, Kingswear, seen above in the 1950s. Maud Mary Ann Ash is listed in the Register of Burials in Kingswear Burial Ground under Entry No.483. She was buried on 16th March 1957: Rev. O'Keefe performed the service. Her occupation was housewife; aged 68. She was buried in an ordinary grave No.469 in the unconsecrated part of the cemetery. She had died in Broomborough Hospital, Totnes, by then much improved and part of the National Health Service, but she might have remembered it as the Union Workhouse. Husband Charles Ash was buried in the same grave on 9th April 1959. Their son, George C. Ash, living at 2, Park View in 1973, was then a ferryman on the Lower Ferry. He died in 1979 and lies in Kingswear Cemetery.

CECIL GEORGE ASHTON
AN EARLY R.A.F. OFFICER

Cecil George Ashton was the son of George Rossi Ashton, a famous artist and illustrator. During his later years George Rossi Ashton lived in Kingswear. His R.A.F. Service Record tells us that Cecil George was born in 1900 in Australia. By 1918 Cecil George Ashton had joined the Australian R.N.V.R. and had been accepted for the Royal Flying Corps. The Royal Air Force (and the Women's' Royal Air Force) were formed on 1st April 1918 by a merger of the Royal Flying Corps and the Royal Navy Air Squadron. Ashton's Service Record, acquired from the National Archives and downloaded via the Internet, is an interesting relic of its time. Untidy, writing almost illegible, notes terse and in jargon; we suspect that it was the work of tired and over-stressed clerks who were more interested in their de-mob dates than their tasks. In May 1918 Ashton was a Lieutenant, temporary Captain in administration. By 16th June 1918 Ashton was stationed at Strathbeg which was an airship base. It is not clear whether he ever learnt to fly. He was posted to Malahide and Llangefni on the North Wales coast.

Airships patrolled from there at this time, as did obsolete Airco DH6 two-seater trainers. They were meant to locate and either report on or drop small bombs on, enemy U-boats lying in wait for Liverpool shipping. Inexperienced pilots were given this job.

Ashton had short postings to London and Wexford during this time. The indistinct handwriting and a cryptic note on his service record mentions airships. The Armistice was signed on 11th November 1918.
In December Ashton was posted to Pembroke, also an airship base. We ask whether he was doing vital liaison work, or was he being given a run-around as a body surplus to requirements? On the 1st January 1919 he was sent to a dispersal centre at Crystal Palace. On 21st January 1919 he was placed on the unemployed list but remained in the RAF. On 24th February he died of influenza and pneumonia at 22 St. John's Wood Park.

The Times carried a notice of his death.
Death - On Active Service - In loving Memory of Capt. Cecil Rossi Ashton, R.A.F., the loved son of Mr. and Mrs. Rossi Ashton, Kingswear.

WILLIAM BELL
KILLED ON THE SOMME

William Bell was the eldest son of John Bell, the foreman of the Kingswear Steam Laundry and his wife Sarah. He was the first of her eleven children. In 1901 William was aged 14 and was working as an errand boy after leaving Kingswear School. His name is with the Bell family on the 1911 census, but without any details. He seems to have been entered in error by his father. William enlisted at Dartmouth and joined the 24th Battalion Royal Fusiliers (City of London Regiment). Private Bell was killed in action on the 13th November 1916 and is buried in Redan Ridge Cemetery No.3, Beaumont-Hamel, Somme, France.

BERNARD AVIS BLACKBOROW
AWARDED THE MILITARY CROSS

Bernard Avis Blackborow appears on the 1911 census as living at Fir Mount, Kingswear. He was the grandson of Thomas Avis the successful Kingswear boat builder and some-time ferry lessee. His mother, nee Ida Avis, had been widowed and had returned to Kingswear from Newport, Monmouthshire, with her seven children.

Bernard was 13 and still a scholar. The Paignton Western Gazette of 9th May 1918 tells us that Second Lieutenant Bernard Avis Blackborow attached to the Royal Horse Artillery in France and younger son of Mrs. Blackborow has been awarded the Military Cross. Bernard survived the war and became Major Blackborow and retired to Stoke Gabriel. He died in 1980 aged 83 and is buried in Kingswear Cemetery.

DOUGLAS BOYD-CARPENTER
KILLED IN ACTION IN FRANCE

Douglas Boyd Carpenter was born in 1888. He was the son of Bishop William Boyd-Carpenter, the famous and highly regarded Bishop of Ripon. The Boyd-Carpenters kept a family home at Riversea, Kingswear, from about 1910 until the death of the Bishop in 1923. Douglas is not yet directly linked to any visit to Kingswear but as his name was included on the Kingswear War memorial he is assumed by us to have visited Riversea from time to time. Lieutenant Douglas Boyd Carpenter, 89th Field Company, Royal Engineers was killed on 29th August 1916 aged 28, and is buried in Delville Wood Cemetery, Longueval. He had married, and by about 1920 his widow had become Mrs. H. C. Pelly of Venars, Nutfield, Surrey.

FREDERICK BREWSTER
KILLED DURING THE BATTLE OF JUTLAND

Although Alfred Brewster was a butler, we do not know at which Kingswear house he worked. He arrived in Kingswear from Harrow, Middlesex, with his family in the summer of 1895 and took one of the Agra Villas on Brixham Road. Our hero was his eldest son Frederick Charles Brewster, who was a scholar at Kingswear School and left in 1898 having reached Standard VI, the highest achievement possible in that school. In 1901 the family was living at No. 3 Overhill; Frederick had four younger sisters. Frederick C. Brewster, aged 16, was apprenticed to a mason. He joined the navy and his intelligence and work bore fruit. The Commonwealth War Graves Commission records that Petty Officer Frederick Charles Brewster R.N. on the cruiser H.M.S. *Indefatigable*, was killed in action at the battle of Jutland on 31st May 1916. The sinking of H.M.S. *Indefatigable* was a tragedy that ought not to have happened. Fleet safety guidelines had not been adhered to. Explosives had been stored all over the ship so that they were available for rapid re-loading of the guns. They should have been kept in the magazines until needed. So when a direct hit ignited the explosives there was a horrendous explosion which sank the ship instantly. Those below decks did not stand a chance and were killed. Kingswear boy Richard Todd was also killed on this ship that day.

HMS Indefatigable

ARTHUR BROOKING
AN INDIAN NAVY COMMANDER EXTENDING THE BRITISH EMPIRE

Arthur Brooking was born in Dartmouth in 1818, twin brother of Julian Brooking. He was living at Kingswear Lodge in the 1871 census and died at Kittery, Kingswear in 1883. He was the brother of John Brooking who lived at Nethway House from 1861. In the 1840s we find him in India intending to make his fortune. As was normal at the time, he took an Indian wife. We hear no more of this lady; maybe she died in childbirth; maybe she was abandoned. The story of this part of his life is unclear, but Brooking Hill, Range Hill Estate, Khadki Pune, seems to bear his name. Arthur acquired skills as a surveyor and navigator. In May 1850 he married his cousin Frances Susan Brooking, at St. John's Calcutta, who had been born in Dartmouth in 1827. They had children. In 1851 the Brookings left India for Burma, with Arthur as captain of the East India Company steamer *Proserpine*.

Our source for the next part of his life is 'The Second Burmese War - A narrative of operations at Rangoon in 1852' by William F.B. Laurie, published in 1853. During the nineteenth century the British Government and people firmly believed that all non-Christian nations were not fully civilised and that they would be better off if their affairs were controlled by Britain. Incidentally their resources could then be exploited for the benefit of the British Empire.

The teak forests of Burma were one of the many resources which British traders coveted. A war was provoked which enabled troops from India to be sent to conquer part of Burma. The army was supported by a squadron of gunboats from the Royal Navy. These boats were to force their way up the Irrawaddy River. Early in the war a joint R.N. and Bengali marine force took Martaban. The *Proserpine* was included in this naval force.

From 1826 the treaty of Yandaboo had guaranteed security of merchants and British commerce during trade with Burma. There was to be no oppression of British subjects. By 1852, either due to lack of diplomacy or deliberate provocation, relationships between the East India Company and the Burmese rulers had deteriorated. All foreigners in Burma came under immediate threat. These anti-western policies induced the East India Company to suppress the "Barbarian Insolence" by force.

The *Proserpine* was sent with some small Royal Navy vessels to Rangoon to cover the evacuation of non-Burmese citizens. The "Friend of India" (a Bengal newspaper) reported that "The Prosperine steamer ran close into the main wharf, and eight or ten of the boats from the frigate and steamers came to the shore to protect and receive the fugitives. Meanwhile the streets were filled with armed Burmese, and Burmese officers were moving to and fro on horseback, threatening all those who gave assistance to the foreigners; in consequence of which, not a coolie would be procured."

All classes of foreigners - Mongols, Mussulman, Armenians, Portuguese and English were seen crowding down to the river with boxes and bundles and whatever they could carry, but they were obliged, generally, to abandon all they possessed. On the 8th January 1852 the *Proserpine* left for Moulmein with upwards of two hundred refugees on board. The next day an open war took place with numerous ships taking part and about 300 Burmese killed. A large squadron of British ships was assembled and prepared for war. Fighting continued, and in April the British steamers *Hermes*, *Rattler*, *Salamander* and the Hon Company's steamer *Proserpine*, were assembled to attack Martaban and bring troops to the chief scene of the action. The *Proserpine* was used to take an interpreter, Captain Latter, with a flag of truce, to inquire if any reply had been received from the Court of Ava to the Governor General's letter. On reaching the stockades which guarded both sides of the river, the steamer was fired on. The cool courage of Commander Brooking was admirable on this trying occasion. He not only extricated the *Proserpine* from danger, but blew up a magazine on shore, which inflicted a severe loss on the enemy.

The month of June became celebrated for the achievements of the *Proserpine* now under the control of the newly promoted Captain Brooking. He took his flotilla up the Irrawaddy River exploring to within thirty miles of Prome, in the heart of the enemy country. The river was shallow, and Brooking had to find ways to get his flotilla over the numerous sandbanks. With the assistance of two well armed boats of HMS *Fox* he captured and destroyed eighty boats of grain of thirty tons each. The rice in these boats was destined for the Burmese army. Brooking was seen to perform his duties "as if he was on the Thames". The *Proserpine* did not escape being fired on and an intelligence report mentioned "a brilliant little affair against the stockade" which she destroyed and, after expending all her ammunition, returned safely.

Brooking Wharf and Brooking Street, Rangoon were named after Arthur Brooking. Frances Susan Brooking died in 1854. On 15th May 1856 Arthur Brooking married Emma; we do not know her maiden name. They had five children; Emma 1855-1915, Gertrude 1857-????, Arthur 1860-1934, Alice 1861-1932, and Cecilia 1864-1954. Alice was born in Rangoon, was educated in a convent and married David Edward O'Connor in the Roman Catholic Cathedral, Rangoon on 9th August 1886. She died on 18th September 1932 at Esperance Hospital, Eastbourne. Cecilia, born 23rd September 1864 in Rangoon, was baptised in 1877 at Holy Trinity Church Rangoon. In March 1891 she graduated at the Medical College, Rangoon, and died on 13th May 1954 at Julianalaan, Helmond, Nord Brabant, Holland.

In 1863 we find Arthur Brooking as Superintendent of the Irrawaddy Steam Navy. In 1871 a new cottage has been erected by T. Short in Kingswear; it has been purchased by Captain A. Brooking. In the 1871 census we find Arthur Brooking, aged 52, pensioned Indian Officer, married and living at Kingswear Lodge. Mrs Brooking is elsewhere. Mary Wise, widow aged 52, is his general servant assisted by her daughter aged 15.

On 4th October 1872 the Dartmouth Chronicle reported that the lad Arthur Brooking, son of Captain Brooking of Kingswear, who met with a very severe accident some three weeks since at Dawlish, is progressing as favourably as can be expected from the severe nature of the injuries he received. One leg has been amputated but the medical men have good hope of preserving the other one. This Arthur Brooking lived until 1934.

In 1873 the Post Office Directory lists Captain Arthur Brooking H.E.I.C.S. as resident in Kingswear. In the 1881 census we find retired Captain in Marines, Arthur Brooking, visiting 88 Lancaster Gate, London. On December 12th 1883 Captain Arthur Brooking died at The Mount, Kingswear, formerly of the Hon. East India Company's Service; aged 65 years. In 1884 we find the will with Codicil of Arthur Brooking, Captain on the retired list of Her Majesty's Indian Navy, was proved at Exeter by Julian Brooking of Kingswear, Gentleman, the brother and sole executer, leaving a personal estate of £5,027/15/-7. In 1915 Emma Brooking died.

RUSSELL ARTHUR BROWN
RIFLEMAN KILLED DURING THE LIBERATION OF BELGIUM

Commonwealth War Graves Commission tells us that Russell Arthur Brown was the son of Frederick Arthur Brown and Nora Elizabeth Brown of Kingswear. Rifleman Brown had joined the Cameronians 9th Battalion (Scottish Rifles). At the age of 30, he was killed on 7th September 1944. He is commemorated at Leopoldsburg War Cemetery, Leopoldsburg, Limburg, Belgium. We have no more information on Russell Arthur Brown as the service records for World War 2 are only released to family members.

RICHARD BUFTON
SAILOR IN THE SEIGE OF SVEABORG

Richard Bufton's Service Record has survived; the first page tells us that Richard Bufton was born in Portsmouth in 1835. He joined the navy as a boy and served on many ships. The website 'Coastguards of Yesteryear' tells us that when Richard was 19 in 1855, he was serving on H.M.S. *Hawke* when, during the siege of Sveaborg, together with the 8 gun H.M.S. *Desperate,* they engaged batteries and gunboats near the mouth of the Dwina River. The naval ships were used to shell the fort. Later *Hawke* and *Conflict* landed parties ashore, destroyed several vessels, and repulsed a body of troops near Dome Ness, at the mouth of the Gulf of Riga.

This campaign was the naval northern front of the Crimean War. The Russian capital of St. Petersburg was constantly threatened, tying up valuable troops which could have otherwise been sent to Sebastopol. Sailors on H.M.S. *Hawke* were awarded the Baltic Medal. In 1859, when he was 24, he married Sarah Ann Marchant, aged 22, at St.Mary's, Portsea, Hampshire. In 1861 he was on H.M.S. *Queen* and was in Beirut, Syria. On 22nd May 1869, he was rewarded for his good service with a post with the coastguards and lived at 6 Church Park

Cottages, Kingswear. In November 1886 we find a paragraph in the Dartmouth Chronicle which reads "On Tuesday evening, about 10 o'clock, a young woman named Mary Opie, cook at the Royal Dart Hotel had a very narrow escape from drowning. It seems she had been at Dartmouth, and on her return two boys took her across the river in a small boat. When she was getting out of the boat at the Kingswear pontoon she fell overboard into the water. Her screams attracted several people to the spot. Amongst the first to arrive were three of the porters at the station, and one of the ferrymen, Richard Bufton, who fortunately was near at hand with his boat. Previous to this one of the boys pluckily dived in after the woman but missed her.

When she was sinking the second time she was caught by the hair of the head, and, with difficulty, lifted into the boat. The two boys then hastily took to their boat, and it was not known who they were. In consequence of their sudden disappearance when the coastguard came on the scene, it is supposed that the boys had stolen somebody's boat to put the woman across. Her hat was picked up off the Yacht Club and the next morning her brooch was found in the ferryboat. She lost half a sovereign, having taken it out of her purse to get change to pay the boys, and was holding it in her hand when she fell into the water. With the exception of the fright we understand that Miss Opie is little the worse for the ducking." Richard stayed in the village until his death in 1914.

RICHARD LAWRENCE LUSCOMBE CAUNTER
KILLED FIGHTING TURKS IN IRAQ

C.W.G.C. tells us that Richard Lawrence Luscombe Caunter was the son of Richard Lawrence Caunter and Mena Caunter of the Priory, Kingswear Devon. He had joined the 7th Battalion of the Gloucester Regiment and had become a second lieutenant. His 7th battalion served in Gallipoli, Mesopotamia and Persia. He was wounded fighting against Turkish troops in Iraq and died of his wounds on 18th December 1916 aged 25. He is commemorated in the Amara War Cemetery.

On her death, Mena Caunter left The Priory, seen above, to the people of Kingswear for use as Old Peoples' Residences.

ARTHUR CLAYTON
DISTINGUISHED SERVICE CROSS

Arthur Clayton was born on 14th October 1903, the son of Sir Harold Dudley Clayton 10th Baronet and Leila Celia Clayton. In 1927 Sir Arthur Harold Clayton, 11th Baronet, married Muriel Edith Lily Clayton, daughter of Arthur John Clayton and Alice Rose Jones. In 1931 Arthur Clayton married secondly Alexandra Andreevsky, daughter of Sergei Andreevsky. From 1939 to 1945 Sir Arthur Clayton fought in the Second World War gaining the rank of Lieutenant-Commander in the service of the Royal Navy Volunteers. He was mentioned in Despatches and was awarded the Distinguished Service Cross. After a divorce he remarried and in 1973 we find him married fourthly to Diana and living at Colonsay, Church Hill, Kingswear.

Topline Broadhurst gave an address at Sir Arthur's Memorial Service held in Kingswear on 24th Sept 1985.
'In World War two Sir Arthur arrived in Kingswear with his M.G.B. for Special Duties. He had the task of taking parties of Special Service soldiers to land in France and the Channel Islands The soldiers would come on board with wicker shopping baskets full of hand grenades. When Arthur got as close as he could to the enemy shore, the soldiers would go off in their rubber dinghies. Arthur would then have to wait to hopefully rendezvous with them several hours later. He was delighted on one night when some German prisoners were brought back in their night-shirts, protesting loudly.

In preparation for D-Day Arthur was promoted to a larger boat with torpedoes, M.T.B.677. He was Mentioned in Dispatches; the citation says:-
"As Commanding Officer of M.T.B. 677, forming part of the force which torpedoed and damaged an Elbing class destroyer on the night 6/7 May 1944, he handled his ship with considerable skill and coolness, less than one mile from the enemy coast in conditions of bright moonlight, and a swell, in shallow waters surrounded by rocks dangerous to navigation. He manoeuvred his ship, undetected by the enemy, into correct position, and had it been necessary for him to fire his torpedo, would have been able to do so with a good chance of hitting the target".

A little later, Arthur was awarded the Distinguished Service Cross for bravery and skill in command on M.T.B. 677 when in action against the enemy on the nights of 26/27 May and 5/6 August 1944. This Commanding Officer is a keen efficient seaman who has been an inspiration to his ship's company and an example to the Flotilla. The citation did not mention the severity of the damage suffered by M.T.B. 677, or the fire aft and the fact that Sir Arthur was standing on top of over two thousand gallons of high octane petrol.

In these actions, our M.T.Bs were attacking very much larger and more heavily armed enemy minesweepers and trawlers as well as E-boats. Arthur was now forty years old and a lot older than the other officers in command of our M.T.Bs as they moved up the English Channel, helping to bottle up the German Navy, night after night, to keep the supply routes open for our advancing army. He finally finished up in Dover and Ramsgate. He referred to all this as "Yachting at the Government's expense". After the war he returned to live in the village he loved.

ANONYMOUS MIDSHIPMAN OF HMS DART
AN AUTHOR'S INVENTION

Most of the tales related in 'The World of Adventure', published in 1895, are true, so the tale of a ship's boat being wrecked on the Mewstone has absorbed a lot of time and mental energy in trying to find some corroborative evidence. With some regret we now conclude that this adventure only happened in the mind of the anonymous author. We wonder whether this tale came from the same pen as Nancy Tarron.

Allegedly, in March 1816, the sloop-of-war *Dart* was in Dartmouth Harbour. We have not found a naval ship of that name existing in 1816; earlier and later vessels bore that name but apparently none were afloat in 1816.

The midshipman who spins the yarn tells us that he was sent to Torbay in the ships long boat, with a crew of eight and an armed marine, to intercept smugglers but found nothing happening. On his return the weather worsened and they struck a rock. Our hero got onto what is assumed to be the Mewstone and after a great and dramatic struggle he got ashore and climbed the cliff, leaving a sailor from his crew to be rescued later on the beach. The others were all drowned. Arriving at a dwelling (which seems to have been Brownstone Farm) his story of shipwreck was not believed at first. Ultimately he received kind treatment and his exhausted colleague was rescued. An enhanced version of this tale was relayed in good faith to our friend Ray Freeman as a true tale handed down in the family, and she repeated it in her booklet on Brownstone. We fear that dear lady swallowed it whole, not being aware of how and where it had been told in print.

JOHN NOEL DOWLAND
AWARDED THE GEORGE CROSS - KILLED ON ACTIVE SERVICE

John Noel Dowland was the son of a one-time vicar of Kingswear, Reverend Frank Michael Dowland, M.C., and Irene Dowland, but now of Ruscombe Vicarage, Twyford, Berkshire. Our twentieth century records have not yet been fully digested so we do not yet have certain proof that John ever visited his father while he was vicar of Kingswear

The London Gazette on the 7th January 1941 stated that Squadron leader John Noel Dowland was awarded the George Cross for his gallantry in defusing a bomb which had fallen on a grain ship SS *Kildare* in Immingham Docks on 11th Feb 1940. The bomb proved difficult to defuse as it was wedged with its nose penetrating through the main deck at an extreme angle. He also displayed "conspicuous courage and devotion to duty in circumstances of exceptional danger and difficulty when defusing a bomb on a trawler" in June 1940. Acting Wing Commander John Noel Dowland, aged 27 years, was killed on 13 January 1942. He is buried in the Commonwealth War Graves Cemetery on Malta. We have no information on the circumstances of his death. We have not yet researched the award of the Military Cross to our one-time vicar of Kingswear.

ALAN DUDLEY, TERENCE SATCHELL, DENNIS THYER
RESCUE IN WATERHEAD CREEK

On Sunday afternoon, 14th May 1944, Dennis Thyer, Terence Satchell and Alan Dudley, with several other boys were swimming in Waterhead Creek, when one of them got into difficulties.
The Dartmouth Chronicle tells us that Edward Hopper, aged eleven and half, who is a strong swimmer, dived under the raft which had been made by local boys. Just as he was emerging from the water, his bathing costume got caught on a nail protruding from the underside of the raft, and he was held fast.

All his struggles to free himself were in vain; and his head was visible for an instant only at a time. Terence Satchell, aged 11, and Alan Dudley aged 12, who saw Hopper's struggles, thought at first he was gaming, but soon realised his peril. They dashed to his assistance and were followed by Dennis Thyer aged 15 years, elder son of Mr. F. C. Thyer of 3 College View. Thyer eventually succeeded in extricating Hopper. They got him to the mud in a very exhausted condition, where after a rest he was able to proceed to his home. Had it not been for the presence of mind and pluck of Dennis Thyer, it is most likely that Hopper would have been drowned. All of the four boys are strong swimmers. Edward Hopper is the son of Mr. Wilfred Hopper of College View, Kingswear and now serving in the army.

The award of the parchment of the Royal Humane Society to three Kingswear boys was announced this week for their part in the rescue of one of their chums who got into difficulties while bathing in Waterhead Creek on Sunday May 14. The award was presented in London on 13th June 1944.
The Scouts Certificate of Gallantry has been awarded to patrol Leader D. Thyer and scouts Terence Satchell and Alan Dudley of the 1st Kingswear Scouts Group in recognition of their gallantry in rescuing Edward Hopper at Waterhead Creek.

Terry Satchell

ALFRED EVANS
SEAMAN TORPEDOED OFF GIBRALTAR

Seaman Alfred Evans, aged 27, serving with the Royal Naval Patrol Service on H.M. Yacht *Rosabelle* was killed on 11th December 1941. His name is on Kingswear War Memorial. He was the son of James Evans and Elsie May Evans of Dartmouth, and husband of Cecile Ellen Evans of Kingswear. H.M.Y. *Rosabelle* left Gibraltar early on 11th December 1941 and was torpedoed shortly afterwards by *U374* after *Rosabelle* had responded to the sinking of H.M.S. *Lady Shirley* by the same U-Boat.

HERBERT FITZHERBERT
DISTINGUISHED NAVAL CAREER WITH PROMOTION TO ADMIRAL

Sometimes we feel that our administrators are anything but heroic, but here we have an example of one who stuck bravely to his work through a great sea battle and rose thereafter through many promotions.

We include him as a tribute to all the administrators of Local History Groups throughout Britain who doggedly provide a framework wherein their colleagues can undertake research. Herbert Fitzherbert was born in 1885 at Kingswear. In 1895 he joined H.M.S. *Britannia*. In 1905 we find that he has just returned to Kingswear after three years service in the flagship *Grafton* on the Pacific station.

The Commander-in-Chief, Captain of the Fleet (Commodore Lionel Halsey), and the Flag Lieut. (Lt-Commander Herbert Fitzherbert) on board H.M.S. *Iron Duke*.

Lieutenant Commander Herbert Fitzherbert, the Flag Lieutenant, on HMS Iron Duke in about 1916.

In 1907 Lieutenant Fitzherbert R.N. left to join H.M.S. *Queen*, flagship of Sir Charles Davey K.C.B., on the Mediterranean Station. In March of 1912 the Dartmouth Chronicle tells us that an interesting little ceremony was witnessed at Bayard's Cove outside the Mission Rooms on Sunday morning. Mrs. Fitzherbert, who was accompanied by Lieutenant Fitzherbert R.N., hoisted a new flag which she had donated to the Bayard's Cove mission. From 1914 to 1916 Herbert Fitzherbert was Flag Lieutenant to the Admiral Commander in Chief. He was on board the flagship during the Battle of Jutland and was Mentioned in Despatches for his work during the battle. In September 1916 he was awarded the Russian Order of St Anne; we have no idea why.

In 1917 he was promoted to the rank of Commander. In the 1919 Honours List Herbert Fitzherbert got the C.M.G. for valuable services while Flag Lieutenant to Admiral of The Fleet, Viscount Jellico of Scapa G.C.B. O.M. G.C.V.O, when Commander in Chief Grand Fleet, and to Admiral Sir Charles E. Maddern G.C.B. K.C.M.G. C.V.O., Second in Command of the Grand Fleet. About 1920 Herbert Fitzherbert married Rachel the second daughter of the late Colonel L. H. Hanbury C.M.G. They had one son, Lieutenant Nicholas Fitzherbert R.N., who died in 1946.

About 1924 an Incoming Passenger List for SS *Merkara*, Ports of departure Bombay via Karachi, Suez, Port Said, Malta and Plymouth, Port of Arrival London, lists Herbert Fitzherbert, aged 36, of Hitcham House, Bucham, Bucks., with Rachel aged 26 and Nicholas aged three. We do not know where they boarded the *Merkara*. From January 1925 to August 1926 we find no appointment listed but in July 1926 Herbert Fitzherbert is the first commanding officer of H.M.S. *Enterprise*.

By July 1926 Herbert Fitzherbert is Flag Captain on H.M.S. *Coventry*, a cruiser, and Chief Staff Officer to Rear-Admiral (D) Commanding Destroyer Flotilla of the Mediterranean Fleet. In March 1929 he was Naval Assistant to the First Sea Lord on H.M.S *President*. In January 1931 he took the Imperial Defence Course at the Imperial Defence College and by January 1932 he was Commander Signal School, Portsmouth, on H.M.S. *Victory*. From 1934 to 1936 he was commanding H.M.S. *Devonshire*, another cruiser, in the Mediterranean but found time during 1935 to be Aide-de-Camp to King George V. From February 1936 to March 1937 he seems to have rested ashore, unless he was engaged in some secret work. In January 1936 Herbert Fitzherbert became a Rear Admiral, while from March to July 1937 he underwent the Senior Officers War Course at R.N. College Greenwich (HMS *President*).

In the Coronation Honours of 1937 he was made a C.B. and from November 1937 until 1943 he was Flag Officer commanding Royal Indian Navy and Naval Adviser to His Excellency the Commander in Chief and Defence Member and Principal Sea Transport Officer, India. In July 1939 he was promoted to Vice-Admiral. In the King's Birthday Honours of 1941 Herbert Fitzherbert received the K.C.I.E. In March 1943 he is listed as Retired, but from April 1944 to June 1944 he was Flag Officer in Charge, Tunisia (HMS *Hasdrubal*). In April 1946 Herbert Fitzherbert is now an Admiral (retired).

VALENTINE FRANCIS GIBBS
BRAVERY AND DEATH DURING THE ZEEBRUGGE RAID

Valentine Francis Gibbs was born in 1882 at Crahanis Town, South Africa. In 1891 he was at school in Clifton, Bristol, while his parents, listed as James R Gibbs, born at Westbury-on-Trym, Gloucestershire, aged 47, a retired Lieutenant Colonel in the army, and Louisa A Gibbs, aged 39, born at St.Albans, Hertfordshire. They were living at 1 Priory Cottages, Kingswear, where they employed four servants living in; Henry Cox, aged 37, was Coachman/Groom together with his wife Eliza, aged 36, and their daughter Maria, aged 20. Their other servant was Laura I Butt from Templecombe, Somerset. We presume that Valentine returned here during his holidays. Valentine entered the Royal Navy as a cadet in August 1897, presumably at Dartmouth. In 1898 he was a midshipman on HMS *Barfleur*. He was injured on the 21st June 1900, while serving on *Barfleur* at the relief of the Legations in Peking during the Boxer Rebellion.

The menacing U-boats of the First World War had a base inland in German-held Belgium. They reached the sea via the Bruges Canal at the port of Zeebrugge. A daring plan was made to block the canal dock gates with three old ships. Zeebrugge was heavily defended but the harbour had to be temporarily controlled while the blockships were put in position. Three old coal-burning cruisers were filled with concrete and sailed across the Channel with minimum crew to be scuttled across the entrance to the canal.

Large numbers of officers and men volunteered to take part in this operation. Valentine Gibbs was a member of the crew of HMS *Tiger* but was given command of HMS *Iris*, a commandeered Mersey ferry boat. Her sister ship was HMS *Daffodil*.

The Iris

Iris and *Daffodil* were to go alongside the outer breakwater (The Mole) and marines would disembark with the intention of destroying the German artillery mounted on the breakwater. The ferries were chosen for their shallow draught which would allow them to sail over the top of minefields and navigate the waters close to the Mole.

Their double hulls made them almost unsinkable and they had an added advantage in that, as ferries, they had been built to withstand constant bumping into quaysides. Being civilian vessels they carried no armoured plating. Seventy six vessels carrying over one thousand seven hundred men took part in the raid. The leading ship was HMS *Vindictive* commanded by Captain Alfred Carpenter which took in tow the two ferries.

As the fleet approached the Belgian coast fast British motor launches threw up a smoke screen which initially went well but at the last moment the wind changed and the smoke cleared, which left the raiders in full view of the defending shore batteries. The British were soon lit up by the Germans firing star shells. Heavy guns immediately opened fire on *Vindictive*, causing much damage and heavy casualties.

It proved impossible to secure *Vindictive* to the Mole using grappling irons and *Daffodil* had to act as a tug and hold her in position throughout the raid. Despite the fact that two German shells exploded in her engine room, the *Daffodil* engineers managed to maintain full steam with her coal-fired boilers. During this difficult manoeuvre her commander, Harold Campbell, was hit in the head by a piece of shrapnel and blinded in one eye, but still remained at his post.

Because *Daffodil* had to hold *Vindictive* in place none of her team could take their places in the raid. As intended *Iris* came alongside the Mole, a few hundred yards ahead of *Vindictive*. *Iris* had difficulty staying close to the harbour wall and was in danger of drifting away, but as she heaved up and down in the swell, Lieutenant Commander Bradford jumped onto the wall. He managed to secure *Iris* to the Mole but as he did so he was hit by gun fire. He fell into the sea between the Mole and the ship. Petty Officer Hallihan dived in to rescue him, but they were both drowned. Most of the marines from the *Iris* did not get on to the Mole because of the difficulty of using scaling ladders and ropes from the ferries heaving deck. Their grappling hooks were not long enough get across the width of the parapet. *Iris* was in full view of the German artillery.

A single heavy shell burst below decks where the marines had been awaiting their turn to go up the gangways. Forty-nine of them were killed out of fifty-six, the remainder being wounded.
The ward-room, which was being used to house the wounded, also received a shell, killing four officers and 26 men. *Iris*'s total casualties were eight officers and 69 men killed and three officers and 102 men wounded.

Valentine Gibbs was hit while on his bridge; both of his legs were shot away. His crew marked the spot where he lay wounded and noted that he had continued to direct his ship in spite of his wounds. Gibbs was obliged to change *Iris*'s position and take partial cover astern of *Vindictive*. He died the next day.

The blockships were scuttled in position and the entrance to the canal was blocked. However British Intelligence had failed to notice that by using another canal the U-boats could still reach the North Sea by a different route.

Two VCs were awarded; they were allocated by raffle when the ships got home. Gibbs did not get one. His shipmates paid for his memorial stained glass window, still to be seen in Kingswear church, which bears the inscription "Remember Commander Valentine Francis Gibbs

B.D. who died in the service of his country at Zeebruge on St. George's day 23 April 1918, to whose memory the officers and men of HMS *Tiger* dedicate this window." B.D. seems to indicate that he had gained a university qualification as Bachelor of Divinity. Valentine is buried in Kingswear cemetery. We have found at least two siblings to Valentine on the 1891 census. Frederick M G. was born in Weston Super Mare 1879 and Herbert T C in Ganhanis South Africa in 1881. Fredrick was named as Valentine's executor. He had been relatively wealthy, leaving effects worth £3,247-15s-3d. Probate at London was granted to Frederick Montague James Gibbs - a transport officer.

THE HAMLYN BROTHERS - CHARLES ERNEST AND HENRY
DIED IN FRANCE ON THE SAME DAY

Charles Ernest Hamlyn and Henry Thomas Hamlyn were born at Starcross in 1888 and 1892. We find them in Kingswear in 1901, aged 14, and 9, living in Brixham Road. Charles was working as an errand boy; Henry (known as Harry) was a scholar. His parents were William and Mary Jane Hamlyn. There were four other siblings.

In 1911 the family was at Roseberry Cottage. Charles was an agricultural labourer and Henry was an apprentice blacksmith. Charles married Ettie Rundell in 1911. They lived in Woodland Terrace, Kingswear. In 1914 Charles volunteered to be put on the army reserve; this was recorded in the Roll of Heroes maintained by the Dartmouth Chronicle. He was called up in due course and became a horse driver with the Horse Transport Army Service Corps and attached to the Guards Division Train.

In 1918 he was wounded and subsequently died on 19th October, aged 30. He is buried in Etretat churchyard in Seine-Maritime, France. Charles Hamlyn left three children. Rose Mary baptised 1912, Ernest Charles born February 1913, Florence Edith born 21st August 1915 and baptised 6th October 1918, thirteen days before her father's death.

Henry Thomas Hamlyn completed his training as a blacksmith and continued his trade in the army, holding the Rank of Shoeing and Carriage Smith, 80th Airline Section, in the Corp of Royal Engineers. He died on the same day as his brother. He is buried in Roclincourt Valley Cemetery.

ARTHUR WILLIAM HARVEY
AWARDED THE MILITARY CROSS

Arthur Harvey was born in Kingswear in 1896. The 1901 Census lists him as living with his parents and siblings at 2 Kingsworth Cottages. His father John, born Diptford, was a G.W.R. Porter. His mother, Elizabeth, was born in St Agnes Cornwall.

Paignton Western Gazette, of 10th January 1918, tells us that the Military Cross was conferred upon Arthur William Harvey of Kingswear. He joined the East Surreys and was attached to the Middlesex Regiment. He was 22 years old and was formerly in the office of Messrs. Collins and Co., shipping agents, of Dartmouth. We have not located the citation for his award. After much search of military records online we have not found any reference to Arthur Harvey.

FRANK HOPKINS
FLEET AIR ARM PILOT WHO BECAME AN ADMIRAL

Wikipedia tells us that Frank Henry Edward Hopkins, K.C.B., D.S.O., D.S.C., D.C., was born on 23rd June 1910, son of a solicitor. Educated at the Nautical College in Pangbourne, he joined the Royal Navy as a cadet in 1927. His first ship was H.M.S. *London*, with duties as a midshipman. After a period in destroyers he qualified as an observer in 1934 and flew with Naval Squadrons based on the carriers *Furious* and *Courageous*. In 1939 he was on the staff of the Naval Observer School at Ford, West Sussex. In 1940 he joined 826 Squadron where he covered the Dunkirk Evacuation. Later that year he operated alongside R.A.F. Costal Command, mine laying and making night bombing raids against targets in France, Germany and the low counties.

In 1940 his squadron embarked in the carrier *Formidable*. Shortly before Christmas they escorted a convoy round the Cape of Good Hope. *Formidable* made her way to the Mediterranean by way of the Suez Canal and was almost immediately involved in flying strikes against the Italian Navy at the Battle of Cape Mattapan. *Formidable* was subsequently damaged in the evacuation of Crete and 826 squadron operated from a shore base, mine laying and taking part in bombardment operations where they pioneered techniques later used by the pathfinders. On 6th December 1941 he took command of 830 squadron in Malta. He had already won the D.S.C. and he added the D.S.O. for an attack on a large enemy convoy supplying Axis forces in North Africa during January 1942. His base, Hal Far, suffered from heavy bombing raids, which cost the squadron several of its swordfish bombers. Hopkins was tireless in leading attack after attack on vessels supplying Rommel's army in North Africa. He helped to send thousands of tons of essential supplies to the bottom of the Mediterranean. Subsequently he was appointed to the staff of the British Air Commission in Washington. He qualified as a pilot in 1944.

He was appointed an observer to the U.S. Pacific Fleet, serving in the U.S. carriers *Hancock* and *Intrepid*. He was present at the Battle of Leyte Gulf. In 1945 he was posted to the staff of the Royal Naval College at Greenwich and in 1947 returned to Washington as the assistant naval attaché. He was awarded the American Legion of Merit in 1948. That year he joined the light fleet carrier *Theses* as Commander (Air) and served with her in the Korean War from October 1950 until April 1951. *Theses* won the Boyd Trophy in 1950 for most outstanding feat of airmanship in that year, and Hopkins was mentioned in dispatches. In 1956 he commissioned the Ark Royal after her long refit and during a highly successful commission took her to the United States for the 350 years anniversary celebration of the founding of James Town. From 1958 to 1960 he commanded Britannia Royal Naval College.

In 1960 he was promoted to Rear Admiral and became flag officer flying training. In 1962 he became Flag Officer Aircraft carriers and was promoted to Vice Admiral. In 1963 he became Deputy Chief of Naval Staff and Fifth Sea Lord. He was promoted to Admiral in 1966, served as C-in-C Portsmouth, retiring from the navy in November 1967. He had been made K.C.B. in 1964. Hopkins was married three times; his second wife was Lois Cook.
He had bought Kingswear Court Lodge while at Britannia Naval College, and lived there until Lois died. He then met his third wife, Georgina Priest, and the house was used more as a holiday home. He was involved in a car crash on Hawaii and died from his injuries on 14th April 1990.

Tessa Gibson adds her personal recollections; 'Michael Gibson laid out his garden at Kingswear Court Lodge and also looked after the house while they were away. They were a great couple and if they were to go away for a long time they would clear out their food cupboard and they would give it to us for the children. Once it contained caviar, but the kids were not happy with that. At Easter the biggest Easter egg they could get would be received. One tale from the village was that when he came down one day to get his paper a car had blocked the exit to Church Hill. He got out of his car and shouted at the offending driver. The witness said they have never seen such a refined gentleman come out with such a full flow of naval language. We found them two of nicest people you could wish to meet'.

HENRY RIEVE HORSEMAN
UNDER AGE RECRUIT KILLED ON THE SOMME

The 1911 census records a 13 year old Henry Rieve Horseman, born in Plymouth, as living at 4 Woodland Terrace with his grandfather. He was 74 year old jobbing gardener Samuel Rieve Horsman. Young Henry was a Gardener's Help. In 1914 the Dartmouth Chronicle Roll of Honour lists Henry as having volunteered for immediate service. Apparently he was 16 years old but was accepted without question and became Private Henry Horsman No. 18425, 8th Battalion, Devonshire Regiment.

On 20th July 1916 he was killed. His body was not found and he is remembered on the Thiepval Memorial, Somme, France.

WILLIAM HINE-HAYCOCK
WORLD WAR II SERVICE IN BURMA AND NEW GUINEA

Somerset and Cornwall Light Infantry Obituaries records that William Hine-Haycock was born at Kittery Court, Kingswear, in 1918 and was educated at Cranford and the Royal Military Academy, Sandhurst. In 1939 he appears on the Kingswear Voters List as William Hine-Haycock of Kittery Court.
The same year he was commissioned into the Somerset and Cornwall Light Infantry and posted to the 2nd Battalion at Blackdown. At the outbreak of World War Two he was appointed Intelligence Officer at Brigade H.Q. and went to France with 4th Division. He saw action in Saar before the retreat through Belgium and France and the evacuation of the British Expeditionary Force from Dunkirk. He was mentioned in dispatches. In March 1941 he sailed for the Middle East with 70th Division and saw action in Palestine, Syria and the Western Desert. Early in 1942 the Division embarked for Singapore which was then under serious threat. Whilst at sea, Singapore fell, so the Division was diverted to Bombay then to Arakan and Burma. During the ensuing retreat he was again mentioned in Dispatches.

At the end of 1942 he was seconded to the Australian Army in New Guinea. After training he served with 2/48th Australian Imperial Force and 24 Combined Maritime Force throughout 1942 on the coast of Papua. On return to India he attended Staff College at Quetta, and after parachute training was appointed Brigade Major to 14 Landing Brigade. He saw further action in Burma. In 1945 he was invalided home. Later he was posted to Schleswig Holstein as Military Secretary to Sir Evelyn Barker, followed by various Staff and regimental appointments in England, Germany, Greece and the Middle East. In 1959 he was promoted to Colonel and in 1964 was appointed Brigade Colonel Light Infantry. In 1967 he was promoted to Brigadier and assumed his last posting as Defence Attaché, Madrid. In 1971 he retired from the Army. In 1973 he is on the Register of Electors at Kittery Court, Priory Street.
He died in September 1989, aged 71.

GERALD DE COURCY IRELAND
WOUND IN FLANDERS

The Dartmouth Chronicle of 3rd September 1915, records that 'the vicar of Kingswear, Rev. de Courcy Ireland, has received information from the War Office that his eldest son, 2nd Lieutenant Gerald B. de Courcy Ireland, of the 14th Battalion, King's Royal Rifles, attached to the 9th Battalion of the same regiment, has been wounded in Flanders. The young officer was repairing the parapet of a trench on Wednesday of last week when he was shot in both legs by a sniper. The bullets have been extracted and Mr. de Courcy Ireland is now in hospital, and, we are glad to be able to state, is making good progress towards recovery.'

JOHN JAMESON LIEUTENANT
BURIED IN KINGSWEAR

In Kingswear Cemetery we have the military grave of Lieutenant John Jameson of the Royal Army Ordnance Corp. He died in May 1946 aged 27. Apart from this we can find no references to this officer. Search of Commonwealth War Graves Commission website returns no trace. Possibly he died of natural causes. Service records of post First World War personnel are only available to close relatives of the servicemen.

WILLIAM VIVIAN JOLLIFFE
TWICE WOUNDED - TWICE GASSED - KILLED IN ACTION

Various censuses tell us that William Vivian Jolliffe was born in born Chester in 1897. He was the nephew of Charles and Frances Jolliffe who lived at various addresses in Kingswear, namely Fern Bank, Longfield and La Scala from about 1895. Charles Jolliffe was a retired Wesleyan Minister originally from Liskeard in Cornwall, who took an active role on Kingswear Parish Council and the Totnes Board of Guardians. William lived at The Warren, Kingswear, with his father. The Paignton Western Guardian of 14th April 1918 tells us that he joined the army during the first week after war broke out and served in the Medical Corps. If he had once held pacifist views these were soon abandoned. By the time of his death he was a Lance Bombardier in The Royal Artillery and Royal Field Artillery. He was twice wounded and twice gassed. He was killed on 24th March 1918 while in charge of an observation party.

He has no known grave and is remembered at Vlammertinghe New Military Cemetery, Leper, West Vlaanderen, Belgium.

HERBERT JONES
AWARDED THE VICTORIA CROSS

Wikipedia tells us that Herbert Jones was born in Putney in 1940 the same year as his parents bought the Grange in Kingswear, where "H" was brought up. He attended school in Sussex and later went to Eton College. When he left school he joined the Army, went to Sandhurst and was commissioned in the Devon and Dorset regiment. In 1972 we find Herbert Jones, The Grange, Castle Road, Kingswear, as a Service Voter. He was promoted to Lieutenant Colonel in June 1979 and transferred to the parachute regiment on 1st December 1979.

During the Falklands War he was in command of the 2nd battalion The Parachute Regiment. His citation in the London Gazette of 8th October 1982 reads:

"On 28th May 1982 Lieutenant Colonel Jones was commanding 2nd Battalion, The Parachute Regiment, on operation in the Falkland Islands. The Battalion was ordered to attack enemy positions in and around the settlements of Darwin and Goose Green. During the attack against an enemy who was well dug in, with mutually supporting weapons sited in depth, the Battalion was held up just south of Darwin by a particularly well-prepared and resilient enemy position of at least eleven trenches on an important ridge. A number of casualties were received.

In order to read the battle fully and to ensure that the momentum of his attack was not lost, Colonel Jones took forward his reconnaissance party to the foot of a re-entrant which a section of his battalion had secured. Despite persistent, heavy and accurate fire the reconnaissance party gained the top of the re-entrant, at approximately the same height as the enemy position. From here Colonel Jones encouraged the direction of his Battalion mortar fire in an effort to neutralize the enemy positions. However, these had been well prepared and continued to pour effective fire onto the battalion advance, which, by now held up for over an hour and under increasingly heavy artillery fire was in the danger of faltering. In his effort to get a good viewpoint, Colonel Jones was now at the front of his Battalion.

It was clear to him that desperate measures were needed in order to overcome this enemy position and rekindle the attack, and that unless these measures were taken promptly, the Battalion would sustain increasing casualties and the attack perhaps would fail. It was time for personal leadership and action. Colonel Jones immediately seized a sub-machine gun and, calling on those around him and with total disregard for his safety, charged the nearest enemy position. This action exposed him to fire from a number of trenches. As he charged up the slope at the enemy position he was seen to fall and roll backward down the hill. He immediately picked himself up and again charged the enemy trench, firing his sub-machine gun and seemingly oblivious to the intense fire directed at him. He was hit from another trench, which he outflanked and fell dying only a few feet from the enemy he had assaulted. A short time later a company of the Battalion attacked the enemy, who quickly surrendered.

The display of courage by Colonel Jones had completely undermined their will to fight. Thereafter the momentum of the attack was rapidly regained. Darwin and Goose Green were liberated and the Battalion released the local inhabitants unharmed and took the surrender of some 1,200 of the enemy.

The achievements of the 2nd Battalion, The Parachute Regiment at Darwin and Goose Green set the tone for the subsequent land victory on the Falklands. This was an action of utmost gallantry by a Commanding Officer whose dashing leadership and courage throughout the battle were an inspiration to all about him."

For these actions, 'Col H' was awarded the Victoria Cross, pictured above. He is also honoured with a blue plaque on Kingswear Lower Ferry slipway.

JUDHAEL
A BOY VASSAL SERVING HIS LORD DUKE WILLIAM AT HASTINGS

In Domesday Book written in 1086, we find that Warin holds Coletone from Judhael. Coletone had clearly been taken out of the land of Woodhuish during late Saxon times. We can still trace its nearly straight boundaries in the field banks of the present day. It was a new settlement in virgin forest. The first holder doubtlessly cut and marketed charcoal to metal workers and the chilled owners of Anglo-Saxon halls. By Domesday the hill-tops had been cleared of timber and fields had been made. Warin had land for two plough teams of oxen which were there. He also had a serf not to be confused with the eighteenth century version of slave. A serf was completely dependent on his lord and had to serve as directed, but just as a sensible owner of a good horse would ensure that it was well fed, fit and breeding well, so a good master would treat his serfs similarly. The son of a serf might become a villein if there was unused land available.

There were also five villeins, the basic farmers of the manor, paying tribute to their lord in kind, and two bordars, probably part-time craftsmen who might have paid a cash levy. To hold Coletone, Warin had to swear allegiance to his feudal overlord, Judhael, who held the town of Totnes from King William and several other country manors as well. Warin has no connection with the later Warren; rabbits were not introduced until a century later. Judhael was evidently of some considerable age when he died, well into the 1100s, whilst feudal Lord of Barnstaple. So we can suspect that Judhael had, as a young soldier, been with William at Hastings. We can also suspect that Judhael had seen hill-top towns in central France, and wanted to manage similar properties. Too young to be trusted with a town in 1067, we find that in 1086 he was well-established at Loddiswell and Totnes, Totnes perhaps being a later award following the death of an unknown older Norman, who had also fought at Hastings. Now the earthworks at Loddiswell Rings seem to be of the Conquest period. A marching camp of William's cavalry army was left behind on their move westwards and perhaps was allocated to young Judhael. He constructed a ring-work and bailey castle in one corner of the now too large cavalry earthwork. The first true motte was not built until 1070 at York.

Judhael may have attempted to create a Mid-France type town on his Devon hill-top. Had the winds blown from the Massif Centrale rather than Dartmoor, he might have been more successful. As was not unusual in William's reign, there was a falling-out between king and vassal, and Judhael lost Totnes. Later the differences were forgotten and Judhael was granted Barnstaple, where he took over an up-to-date true motte with its bailey.

JAMES HENRY KING
KILLED IN BURMA

James Henry King is named on Kingswear War Memorial. Commonwealth War Graves Commission tells us that he was the son of James Summers King and Violet Elizabeth King of Okehampton. As a lance corporal he was serving with the 1st Battalion Devonshire Regiment in Burma and was killed on 21st April 1944, aged 23. He is commemorated at Rangoon Memorial, Taukkyan War Cemetery, Myanmar. We have noted twenty-three persons with the name King on Kingswear documents between 1838 and 1972 but cannot yet relate James Henry to any one of them.

CHARLES FREDERICK KNAPMAN
KILLED WHILE THE ROYAL NAVY WERE SUPPORTING TOBRUK

HMAS Parramatta

The name of Charles Frederick Knapman is recorded on Kingswear War Memorial. He was the son of Charles Frank and Minnie Knapman of Kingswear. He was born in 1920 and joined the Royal Navy. He was killed on 27th November 1941 while serving as a Stoker 1st Class on H.M.A.S. *Parramatta*. His Majesty's Australian Ship *Parramatta* was a Grimsby class sloop. She was laid down on 9th November 1938 at the Cockatoo Island Dockyard at Sydney, New South Wales and powered by steam turbines. She was commissioned into the Royal Australian Navy on 8th April 1940 and soon commenced duty as a convoy escort. Parramatta was escorting transport ships resupplying the Allied garrison at Tobruk, when she was torpedoed and sunk on 27th November 1941. There were twenty four survivors, but 138 men, including all the officers, lost their lives.

JOHN SETON KYFFIN
ROYAL NAVY - KILLED IN ACTION DEFENDING THE SUEZ CANAL

John Seton Kyffin was born in 1919, the son of John Trevor and Margaret Joyce Kyffin. The Times of 19th August 1940 announced the engagement between Sub Lieutenant John Seton Kyffin R.N., elder son of Captain and Mrs Kyffin and Catherine Mary, second daughter of Major and Mrs. H. M. Richards of Caernywch, Dolgelly. They were subsequently married. John Seton Kyffin had joined the Fleet Air Arm and was operating out of HMS *Grebe*. This was the Royal Navy designation for the pre-war Alexandria airport, known as *Dekheila*, during its use in World War II as a shore base for aircraft of the Fleet Air Arm. The Times on 24th December 1941 bore notice of the death of Sub Lieutenant John Seton Kyffin R.N. beloved husband of Catherine and son of Captain and Mrs Kyffin, Ridley House, Kingswear.

EDMUND LIPSCOMBE
WOUNDED - HIS FOOT BLOWN TO PIECES

Edmund Lipscombe was born in February 1892. He was admitted to Kingswear School on 1st April 1895. In 1901 he was living with his parents, William and Mary Jane Lipscombe, and two older siblings at 5 Church Park Cottages. On 8th October 1915 the Dartmouth Chronicle reported that Private Edmund Lipscombe of Kingswear, serving with the 8th Devon's (Bullers Own), was wounded during the recent Franco-British advance, and is now at Salford Royal Hospital, Manchester. In a letter to his sister Elizabeth, he stated "there were sixteen of us sent to bomb a German trench and we bombed them out of it, but they started to bomb back. I was the leading man all the time when the Huns caught me. When I got back to the end of the trench the Huns caught me right under the boot with a bomb and blew my foot, boot and all, to pieces, so you can tell what it is like. I didn't tell you I was left twelve hours on the battlefield before they carried me in. We started this battle last Saturday at six and it wasn't an half an hour before they were giving themselves up in thousands." In 1939 Mr. and Mrs. Edmund Lipscombe were living at Carlton Lodge. Edmund Lipscombe died age 69 in 1961 and is buried in Kingswear Cemetery.

EVAN HENRY LLEWELLYN
WOUNDED IN SOMALIA

Evan H. Llewellyn was the son of Llewellyn Llewellyn, Justice of the Peace for Devon, who was born at Margam, Glamorgan, and his wife Rose, born at Exeter. They had come to live in a grand style with five servants at Nethway House before the 1881 census was taken. The 1881 census shows them living at Priory House, Kingswear, still with three servants.

Evan H. Llewellyn, born 1872, the eldest of their three children, was by then a Military Cadet. By 1901 Evan Llewellyn was a Captain in the Inniskilling Fusiliers and was attached to the Second Battalion of the King's African Rifles. He was sent to Somaliland from Central Africa in 1902 and was present, with three companies of the Regiment, at Erigo, when the Somali Regiments deserted the British in September of that year. These three Companies were the only regular troops present and undoubtedly saved Colonel Swayne's army from a terrible massacre. The Second Battalion of the Kings African Rifles bore the brunt of the fighting against the Dervishes during 1903 where they lost a quarter of their men, and many of their officers.

The Dartmouth Chronicle for January 15th 1904 carried a despatch from General Egerton to the Secretary of State for War. 'We advanced this morning twelve miles to Jidballi. Our strength is 2,200 regulars and 1,000 irregulars. Jidballi was held by 5,000 Dervishes. The mounted troops were sent out to envelop the enemies' right. Our infantry advanced to within 70 yards of the Dervishes when the Dervishes advanced to charge, but they could not face the frontal fire of our infantry and the flank attack of the mounted troops. The enemy broke and fled, pursued ten miles by the mounted troops. It is estimated that about 1,000 Dervishes were killed, the most in retreat; also many prisoners were taken. 400 rifles have been taken and more are being collected. Among the officers severely wounded is Captain Evan H. Llewellyn of Oversteps, Kingswear.'

From the Chronicle of 13th December 1907 we find that Captain E. H. Llewellyn, son of the late Mr. Llewellyn Llewellyn of Nethway, and Mrs. Llewellyn of Oversteps, Kingswear has been granted the temporary rank of Lieutenant-Colonel whilst employed as commandant of the King's African Rifles. In 1914 Kelly's Directory lists Captain Evan Henry Llewellyn at Nethway House and in 1919 he was there again, but with the rank of Major. In 1923 he was a Brigadier General having been awarded the D.S.O.
In 1935 he was D.S.O. and J.P. Our latest record found so far is from the Dartmouth and Kingswear Directory for 1939 when he was still Brigadier General living at Nethway with Mrs. Llewellyn.

JOHN M. LLEWELLYN
WOUNDED IN FRANCE

John M. Llewellyn was the younger brother of Evan Henry LLewellyn. He was a Captain in the 1st Battalion Devonshire Regiment, son of

Mrs. Llewellyn of Oversteps, Kingswear. The Dartmouth Chronicle reported that he was wounded by Huns during the great advance on the 23rd May 1915.

WILLIAM F. MOIST
RESCUED A BOY FROM DROWNING

William Moist was born in Kingswear in 1869, the son of an agricultural labourer. In 1871 the family was living at 12 High Street, Kingswear. In 1879 10-year-old William, with other boys, was up before Churston Magistrates for stealing apples from Mr. Ellis' orchard at Hoodown Farm. They got eight stripes with the birch rod at the police station in Brixham. On 2nd February 1880 Kingswear School logbook records that two of his siblings died within a week. On 12th February William Moist "did something to the latch of the school gate so as to prevent it lifting. Several children were marked absent although they came in later by the back way." On 5th December 1881 we read that "William Moist has left, aged 14, gone to work. His attendance was always bad so the loss is small." By 1891 he is an "engineer" living with his parents at 1 Laundry Cottages. In 1901 we find him married, with three children, living in the slum of College View. He is a steam launch driver.

In 1911 the family is at Hillside and William is a seaman on a yacht. The Dartmouth Chronicle of 4th September 1914 notes that "A smart rescue from drowning was effected at Kingswear on Sunday morning. George Pollard, the six-year-old son of Mr. Alfred Pollard, accidentally fell from the jetty into the river, and Mr. William Moist, fully clothed, immediately jumped in after him and succeeded in rescuing him, keeping him afloat until the arrival of a boat in which he was taken ashore. Mr. Moist is to be warmly commended for his action." William died in 1929, aged 60, and is buried in Kingswear cemetery.

Kingswear Quay in about 1950

THOMAS NICHOLS
SERVED IN THE BALTIC CAMPAIGN OF THE CRIMEAN WAR

We have the Service Record of Thomas Nichols which tells us that he was born in Kingswear in 1820, but the Kingswear Church Register of Baptisms does not contain his name. We have not searched Brixham or Dartmouth records. Thomas joined the Royal Navy on 28th February 1854 when it was noted that his height was 5 ft 3 3/4 inches; complexion: dark; hair: brown; eyes: hazel; marks: crucifix on left arm.

Perhaps he had been in the merchant navy. He volunteered for seven years service. During the Russian (Crimean) War 1854-1856, he was a Rating AB, and Captain of the Fore Castle on H.M.S. *Miranda*. *Miranda* was a modification of the Royal Navy's first screw sloop, *Rattler*. She was designed with a two-cylinder horizontal single-expansion geared steam engine developing an indicated 613 horsepower and driving a single screw. This was sufficient to achieve 10.75 knots under engines alone. Originally built with fourteen 32-pounder carriage guns in a broadside arrangement, a further 68-pounder pivot gun was added in 1856. In the autumn of 1854 a squadron of three British warships, led by *Miranda*, left the Baltic for the White Sea where they shelled and destroyed Kola. An attempt to storm Archangelsk proved abortive, as was the siege of Petropavlovsk in Kamchatka. Whilst the Anglo-French naval squadron successfully shelled the town, a landing of 800 sailors and marines was repulsed.

We do not know if Thomas was in the shore party or was working the guns on ship. On 3 June 1855 at Taganrog, in the Sea of Azov, two of his shipmates, boatswain Henry Cooper and Lieutenant Cecil Buckley, landed and destroyed equipment and set fire to government buildings despite the town being under bombardment and garrisoned by 3,000 Russian troops. For this action the pair was awarded the first gazetted Victoria Cross. Thomas left the Navy in June 1860.

REGINALD PERRING
KILLED IN BURMA

Reginald Perring appears on the 1939 list of Kingswear voters, living at 3 Higher Street. He was the son of Charles Henry and Mary Ellen Perring and the husband of Phyllis Perring nee Laskey of Kingswear. He was a corporal in the 1st Battalion Devonshire Regiment and was killed, aged 34 on 8th May 1944 while serving in Burma

He is commemorated at Rangoon Memorial, Myanmar, Taukkyan War Cemetery.

PHILIP
HOLY MAN FROM FRANCE WHO MIGHT HAVE ACHIEVED SAINTHOOD

Philip was buried beneath the floor of the chancel in Kingswear church. We estimate that he lived approximately from 1210 to 1270. At the time of his arrival from France this church was still a manorial chapel belonging to the manorial lord of Woodhuish manor; he would have been employed by this Woodhuish lord and would have ultimately been considered as one of the lord's servants in his extended household. Trained in France, and fluent in French and English, he would have been aware of the new polyphonic music being sung in the rebuilt French cathedrals.

He may have been one of the Dominicans or Black Friars who first came to England in 1221. The order quickly spread; they were a teaching and preaching order. We speculate that Philip was a preacher whose words and music were popular and well-received locally. Kingswear church was rebuilt just before the middle of the thirteenth century, perhaps at the time of the ecclesiastical re-organisation of southern England into parishes with nominally resident priests and clearly defined boundaries. St. Mary's Brixham was designated the parish church for the whole of our peninsula. Kingswear and Churston were outlying chapels at this time. Our new church was in the Early English style, with two aisles and an arcade of two-cantered arches. Its tower, much altered, still survives. Windows were now large enough to let in useful amounts of daylight. It was designed to be a good hall in which to preach, and to have good acoustics for the new ecclesiastical music. We speculate that

Philip was its designer and first incumbent. The chapel was intended to serve a good deal of passing trade as well as the local inhabitants. Travellers using the old Kingas Way (or Wayar) from Exeter and onwards as far as Cornwall would cross by ferry here. Even if the boat and boatman were sound, this felt like a big adventure for most travellers. A splash of Holy water and a kind word from Philip would earn a coin in the offertory box. Similarly mariners setting out to sea or arriving safely would beach on the ferry beach and seek reassurance for themselves and their cargos from Philip, again leaving an appropriate offering. Totnes merchants had an interest in the chapel via Totnes Priory.

With lively preachings, a good singing voice in church and around the village, a connoisseur of French wines and a reassuring personality, he may have been a pop-star of his day. It is possible, if he was not a member of the Dominican Order but sympathetic to their ideals, that he was, quite legally in England, married. About 1270 someone with money liked him enough to pay for a reasonably elaborate tomb with a table-top slab carved with a simple cross-fleury. An inscription in Norman French around the bevelled top edge reads in Norman French 'Vous ke ci venez pour la Alme Philip priez: XXX jurz de pardom serra vostra guerdon.' This translates as 'You who come here pray for the soul of Philip: Thirty days of pardon shall be your reward'. Thirty days less in purgatory was an offer worth accepting. It could only have been made by the priest who succeeded him.

Strictly a Dominican ought not to have been honoured in this way but his followers and survivors wished to honour the memory of their friend and tutor. His friends would visit his tomb to ask his help in matters of religion and daily life. Some perceived his interventions as successful. They added doubtlessly valuable inlaid metal panels in gilt, bronze and fine (probably Limoges) enamels. An iron framework with a rounded top was added, over which a fine cloth cover could be draped during Lent. If his fame had reached nobility or bishops he might have begun the process leading to sainthood, but his sailors, farmers and a few small-town merchants could not ensure his lasting fame. Gradually he was forgotten, his brass and enamel inserts were taken, at the Reformation or even before. This old popish relic was dumped in the churchyard by the re-builders of the 1840s. Wisely it has now been brought in from the weather.

JOHN HENRY RUTTER
KILLED WHILE HE WAS A PRISONER OF THE JAPANESE

The name of John Rutter is on the Kingswear War Memorial. We presume that this is the same person whose birth was registered as John H. Rutter in 1914 in the Totnes district. His mother's maiden name Rutter. John had been cared for at the Brixham Boys Home, and left to work at Kingston Farm. David Williams records, in 'Kingston Farm and its Cottages', that he moved to work at Nethway House as a pantry man to Mrs. Llewellyn, and later he became an under footman at Waddeton Court, Stoke Gabriel. The Kingswear Electoral Roll for 1939 lists Elizabeth Rutter, living at 3 Brixham Road.

On 6th March 1947 the Paignton Western Guardian carried an advert "Rutter - In proud and loving memory of Jack, who was lost at sea on or after 5th March 1943, whilst P.O.W. in Japs Hands. Always in the thoughts of Mother, Sisters, Brother-in-law, nephews and nieces, 3 Brixham Road Kingswear."

We find that the Commonwealth War Graves Commission records John Henry Rutter, Lance Bombardier, Royal Artillery, 35 Lt. A.A. Regt. killed on 5th March 1943, son of Elizabeth Rutter; husband of Elizabeth Lorraine Rutter of Bassaleg, Monmouthshire.

A Japanese Hell Ship

We deduce that he had been a prisoner of war and was being transported for slave labour on a so-called Japanese Hell Ship, battened down in its hold. Allied forces had no idea what the cargo was in these, plainly enemy, cargo ships, and sank them as legitimate targets.

CHARLES EDWARD RYDER
SIXTEEN YEAR OLD BOY SAILOR

We discover that Charles Edward Ryder aged 9 in 1911, was the youngest child of Charles and Mary Ryder living at Reservoir Terrace, Kingswear. He had planned a career in the Navy, and had been accepted as a Boy 2nd Class and was training at Plymouth on the old H.M.S. *Powerful*, now or shortly, to be re-named H.M.S. *Impregnable*. At the age of sixteen and a half years he died, apparently of natural causes, in the Naval Hospital at Plymouth on 27th October 1918. He is buried in Kingswear cemetery, and his name is on the Kingswear War Memorial.

HMS Impregnable

GEORGE SATCHELL
ACTIONS AND ILLNESS IN THE CAMEROONS

George Satchell was born in Bristol in 1889. We find him in 1895 being admitted to Kingswear School, the son of Charles Satchell, steam crane driver, of Woodland Terrace, Kingswear. George left school in 1903 having passed Standard VI. The Dartmouth Chronicle of 16th April 1915 tells us that Mr. George E. Satchell, Royal Naval Reserve of HMS *Challenger*, who was invalided home through an attack of malaria, is now on convalescence leave. He has seen plenty of active service fighting the Germans in Africa.

The Chronicle describes the actions of British sailors fighting ashore in the jungle, where the Germans had resorted to mounting their machine guns in trees. *Challenger* was bounced over a sandbank in the river and took several German steamers as prizes.

ROBERT HAYNE SEALE
DECLINE OF A KINGSWEAR CURATE

Robert Hayne Seale was born in 1788. He was a member of the Hayne and Seale families which were prominent in the history of Dartmouth. We have not yet researched his life, or family connections, before 1818. His private notebook or diary covering 1818-1819 has been placed on the Dartmouth History Group website. It was never meant to be seen by anyone other than the author himself. We can deduce that he had been to a university and had obtained a degree in theology.

From his phonetic spelling we can deduce that he favoured the affected drawl of the well-to-do varsity students. His diary is a re-used notebook; pages have been torn out, but we can tell that he had been on a Grand Tour through France and Italy. He came to live in Dartmouth, but was appointed curate, perhaps of Brixham, but we find him taking services at Townstal and Kingswear.

Selected diary entries read:
Tuesday, 3rd November, 1818, went to Exon to be licenced to Kingsware (sic) curacy.

Passage of horses -- £--/-1/--
Lent Charles ------- £--/-2/--
Luncheon at Newton - £--/-3/-6
Boy ---------------- £--/--/-6
Coach to Exon ------ £--/-5/-6
Porter ------------- £--/--/-6
Cowpers Poems ------ £--/16/--
Pocket book -------- £--/-4/--
Knee caps* --------- £--/-7/--
* The damp floor of Kingswear church before its rebuild.
Gloves ------------- £--/-2/--
Total -------------- £-2/-2/--

Wednesday 4th November, 1818
Breakfast with Mr Turner.
To Turner for Licence to Kingsware - £10/15/--
Pouch to Henry at Ottery ---------- £--/10/-6
Postchaise to Ottery -------------- £-1/-5/--
Boy ------------------------------- £--/-4/--
Total ----------------------------- £12/14/-6

Thursday 5th November 1818
Very cross and disrespectful to Granville and my brother John. Spoke imprudently to J. Winsor. Stirring up strife and division by my complaints of my brothers servants. Arrived at Mt. Boone.

Friday 6th November 1818
Wrote Mr. Leigh - Savings Bank - desiring him to inform me whether I had not paid him a £5 note instead of a £1 in subscription to the Missionary Society. My intemperance has caused me to spit blood this day.

Saturday 7th November
Last evening took a blue pill. Spent the morning in my room; spit no more blood.

Sunday 8th November
Mr. Lee writes that I am mistaken as to my having paid £5 for one pound. Mr, Adams did duty for me at Townstal. John Puddicombe is of opinion all my disorder lies in the digestive organs, so think I.

Monday 9th November
Indoor day; purge; took physic. Wm. H. rode Ching (Ching is his 'pony'); had a wet ride home at night.

Selected sequence of entries from various dates:-
Went to Kingsware - Called on Mr. Roope, Mr. Mathews etc.
Agreed with John Heath, who is to groom my pony, for 3s per week.
Did not drink tea with Miss Anderson as she was engaged.
Did service at Townstal forenoon and at Kingsware afternoon.
Paid old Saml. Edwards for rowing me over to Kingsware £--/-1/--.
Rode to Brixham upon a commission.
Buried a corpse at Kingsware at 1/2 past nine.
Called at Fuge - Uncle was rode out.
Received Calvin's Institutes from Ld. R.S.
Christened Robert Putt at Kingsware.
Rode to Norton and afterwards met Mrs B. on the Dittisham Road in her phaeton; mean to speak to her de matrimonio.
Called on Miss Hutchins and paid subscription to the day school.
Mr. Newman gave me a Cardinal Bird.
Monsr. Simon came and gave me his first lesson in Italian.
Wrote Mr. Neck about my Petrox school.
Must have Sam. Edwards and my fathers boat next Sunday.
Performed service very ill.
I wrote Orlando Manley and asked if he knew any eligible curate for Kingsware.
Miss Browne came to Mount Boone.
Began Dr. Stewart's plan of Lavation and Chaffing.
Went to Kingsware - Heard the children their catechism.
Miss Browne returned to Norton.
Quarreled with my sister about Mrs. Marriot's book.
Mr. Neck and Mr. P. came - Brought me Cecil's remains and a Book on the duties of a clergyman.
Paid Col. Seale the sum of £12/10/-- for my own board and £-3/-6/-8 for John Winsor's board and lodging.
I rode to Fuge to dinner - Slept the night - Refused to play cards.
Rode to Blackauton with my uncle Hayne - Returned to So-town: dined there on water-gruel.
Preached at Townstal in ye morning - At Kingsware in the evening.
Desired Mr. Parge at Kingsware to recommend me about six of the most deserving boys of the school.
I mean to give them rewards at Xmas.
Am afraid I spit a little blood this evening.
Increased my cough - Continued to spit bloody mucus.
My symptoms are quite alarming.
Great source of inquietude is intemperate eating and suffocating the Digestions.

Breakfasted in my own room which is infinitely better than going down to breakfast.
Thus one loses no time, nor does one overeat oneself.
J. Puddicombe wrote me a Certificate of ill-health.
Rode to Southtown - Found the cold air affect my cough.
Putting my feet in hot water I find of service.
O. Manley sent me a very good and sensible letter about the school and about my own near prospect of death.
Paulina and I had a long argument on religion - May it avail her some thing!
J. P. called and desired me to eat a broil for breakfast.
Saw Miss Venning and took care to bow to her.
Mr. Adams served Townstal for me: Took physic.
Mrs. Vernon writes - Desires I will go to Churston when I please; mentioned Mrs Mills having written her complaints of me.
Wrote Mrs. Vernon and desired her to recommend me a pupil.
Said I had no resentment against Mrs. Mills so waved all discussions.
Performed services at Kingsware: Communion, did no evening service there.
I breakfasted at Southtown: Went to Kingsware.
A large party dined here - I withdrew at 9 and went to bed.
Performed the service ill, too fast and read without feeling. The sermon I gabbled over terribly.
Debated with my brother and sister on religion; they seemed in a more serious mood. Intemperance of eating and conversation.
I put by 5/- each day to be expended in forfeits for every violation of this rule. These forfeits to be given in charitable donation to Nurse Way.

Robert Hayne Seale died, aged 31, in June 1819, and is buried at Townstal.

REGINALD ERNEST SELWAY
MEDICAL CORPS - AWARDED THE MILITARY MEDAL

Reginald Ernest Selway was born in 1878. On 24th April 1915, at Fovant, he enlisted as a private in the Royal Army Medical Corps. On 9th April 1918 he performed, while working as a stretcher bearer, an act of bravery for which he was awarded the Military Medal. The citation reads
"On the morning of April 9th 1918, there was a heavy barrage at the time through which he had to pass as runner. After giving his message he fainted but immediately recovered and at once returned to his post although the shelling was intense. At this time as well as on other occasions he has shown great courage and devotion to duty."

On 27th March 1919 he received his demobilization account.
Balance due to soldier on arrival at demobilization station £4/11/9
28 days furlough at 2/8d ------------------------------- £3/14/8
28 days ration allowance ------------------------------- £2/18/4
Allowance for plain clothes ---------------------------£2/12/6

War gratuity --£22/-/-
Total -- £35/17/3

He returned from France to Exeter but moved to Kingswear. The voters list for 1939 shows him living, with his wife, Elsie Gladys, at 5 Orchard Terrace, Lower Contour Road.
They were still there in 1973.

THOMAS SHORT
RESCUED A HOUSEMAID FROM DROWNING BUT LOST HIS OWN LIFE

The spot where Thomas Short drowned

Dartmouth Chronicle reports that on Saturday 22nd July a gloom was cast over this town and Kingswear, as the news became generally known that Mr. Thomas Short, a much respected builder of the latter place, had lost his own life whilst trying to rescue a female servant, in the employ of Colonel Maitland of Kingswear Castle, who had fallen overboard.

The facts of this melancholy case will best by known by the following evidence taken at the inquest which was held before H. Mitchelmore Esq., County Coroner, at the Steam Packet Inn, of whom Mr. Paddon, station-master was chosen foreman. Thomas Langmead Casey deposed that he was a carpenter and resided at Kingswear. He knew the deceased and had been a companion of his for nearly 60 years. The unfortunate man was a mason and builder. Both himself and deceased were working near Kingswear Castle.

On Saturday 22nd inst, he saw him shortly after two o'clock, when he was making a hole for a bolt. The next time he saw him, which was after a lapse of a few minutes, was in the water. He heard deceased call "Casey a rope", and went to his assistance. He did not know how the deceased had got into the water; but when he saw him he was quite erect, supporting a female.

Witness then called the assistance of a strange gentleman and by their united efforts succeeded in cutting a piece of rope which formed a portion of a fence. The deceased and the woman were about 5 feet from the steps and in about 8 feet of water. Witness seeing that it was helpless called for his wife to help. One end of the rope was thrown to Short, the woman grasped it but Short did not. Witness thought both had hold of the rope and with the assistance of the gentleman hauled away. When pulling the woman to shore, it was found the deceased had not got hold of the rope, but hold of the woman's dress. The woman being somewhat able to help herself, witness's attention was paid to the deceased. Witness was given the rope by the gentleman and put it under the deceased arms and held him half out of the water. Witness himself sat in about a foot of water. The witness said it was impossible for him with the help at hand to carry the unfortunate man up the steps. Owing to his not seeing any further assistance, he told the gentleman to hold deceased as he had done, whilst he went to Kingswear Castle for help, but there was none to be found. He returned to the scene.

Presently however, a boat came from Dartmouth Castle; the deceased was put on board and conveyed to the ferry slip and thence to the Pitt's Steam Packet Inn and subsequently to his residence. On the landing slip, a gentleman who announced himself as a physician, give directions with a view to recover life and his orders were strictly carried out; deceased arms were exercised and his limbs rubbed with a flannel but all was in vain. The gentleman who assisted in the boat pronounced life extinct. Mr R. Soper, surgeon of Dartmouth was in attendance almost immediately but by request proceeded to Kingswear Castle to attend the servant. Witness sobbed aloud at times while giving evidence.

Sarah Ellis, on being sworn in, stated she went to the water's edge to wash her hands as she had been in the habit of doing. She was standing on the last step out of the water when her foot slipped and she fell in. She screamed once and the deceased came to her assistance, but how he got in the water she could not tell.

The Coroner, in summing up, said the deceased's bravery and humanity deserved the attention of the Royal Humane Society. He was not aware if the Society granted medals to the dead.

The jury returned a verdict of "Accidentally Drowned". We suggest that death was due to natural causes due to the stress of being in the water. The deceased, who was the Vicar's churchwarden for many years, was interred in the church yard, when Rev. J. Smart read the burial service in a very impressive way.The funeral cortege numbered over 100. We have tried to find out more about Sarah Ellis, but we can find no trace of her in any records.

NANCY TARRON
FANTASY OF A KINGSWEAR EXILE

A story titled "The Village Heroine, A True Story of Kingswear" began on page 3 of the Dartmouth Chronicle on 6th May 1898, and was continued over two subsequent editions. Surprisingly the tale has been accepted as true by some local people in recent years. This writer (T.J.M.) knew enough about nineteenth century history to be certain from the outset that what we were being presented with was either fiction or a massively misunderstood version of the truth.

The yarn begins in November 1824 with a Nancy Tarron, portrayed as a young married woman who had recently given birth, and who was also a rowing member of the crew of a local pilot boat, running from her Kingswear home to take her place at an oar. (Women were not unknown on ships of this period, but they were more likely to be pulling on their drawers than pulling on their oars.)

In a storm, two pilots raced to the harbour mouth to get the job of bringing in a damaged vessel which was also flying the quarantine flag. Against orders from her skipper, Nancy went aboard the afflicted vessel and began to nurse the plague-stricken captain, his crew, and the captain's wife. Many details follow, including her time on the Quarantine Hospital Ship, but the infuriated skipper of the pilot boat had Nancy up in court for mutiny.

To help the tale along she was found guilty and sentenced to death. Great indignation was felt in Kingswear, and a petition was sent to London for her reprieve. Eventually Nancy is grudgingly forgiven, and the tale ends when she is visited in her Kingswear home by the widow of the skipper of the plague-ridden ship, who has now married her dead husband's first mate.

The full analysis of the pages of the Dartmouth Chronicle being attempted by TG and TJM has located a paragraph, without a headline, on page 2 of the same edition. "The writer of the 'Village Heroine' is Mr. J. H. Langdon, Home Lea, Polsham Road, Paignton. We received the copy from Mr W. H. Rees, J.P., and an old friend of his. Without wishing to anticipate we may add that the remainder of the tale, which contains nothing but fact, should be of unusual interest to this locality, and to Kingswear in particular." By such remarks many newspapers have lost their credibility.

If there were any truth in the story there ought to be Court Records of the trial, the Petition with many local names, and the Royal Pardon. We have not wasted our time seeking these documents. Should anyone find them the authors will have to apologise!

The pages of The Times for 1824 and 1825 have been read via the internet; Nancy and her story are never mentioned. Clearly there is much accurate Kingswear background to the plot, so let us investigate the author. James Henry Langdon was baptised in Kingswear church on 20th May 1817. He was the son of John Langdon, merchant, and his wife Mary.

In 1841 we find him living as a lodger in the Ship Inn in Lower Street (sic). He is 23 and works as a clerk. In 1851 he is in Palace Street, Holy Trinity Parish, Exeter, a general merchant and now, aged 32, married to Jane, who had been born in Dartington, and with their nine month old daughter Emily Jane. Nephew Charles E. J. Dyson, aged 12 and born in Lisbon, Portugal, lodges with them.

By 1861 he is in London at 3 South Grove, West Highbury, and a Commission Merchant. Emily has now born five daughters and a son. We cannot trace them in the 1871 census, but in 1881 he is in Loughton, Essex living at High Road, Kings Head, Loughton. Now aged 62 James is a Wine Merchant. Four unmarried daughters and a son are at home with their parents.

1891 finds them still at Loughton where they have named the house 'Kingswear'. James H. Langdon is 78 a retired Merchant. Jane Langdon is now described as a Naturalized Portuguese Subject; we assume a mistake. Soon after this Jane must have died and he remarried and moved to Paignton. In 1898 he presented 'The Village Heroine' to the Dartmouth Chronicle.

In 1901 he was 83 and was still living at Holmlea, Polsham Road, but now with wife Emma Langdon, aged 52. They had a visitor, Ann Glanfield, aged 78 of her own means, born Colchester. A real Nancy was born in Kingswear in 1794, but we do not know her maiden name. James Langdon was 21 years her junior. Before 1814 she had married John Talling, a mariner, of Kingswear. Their children were baptised in Kingswear church in 1814, 1816, 1821 and 1829. Perhaps James Langdon phantasized an older woman.

Life did not go well for real Nancy; we find her as a widow aged 57 working as a nurse, perhaps a midwife, at 29 South Street, Tormohun, living-in with a veterinary surgeon and his grocer wife. In 1861 Nancy Talling, born Kingswear, was a lodger in St. Pancras, London. In 1871 she was living at 20 Fortress Grove, St. Pancras, aged 82, Lodger, Pauper (outdoors).

Might James Langdon have been keeping a watchful eye on her, and swapping old tales of Kingswear in the good old days?

FREDERICK HOWARD THOMPSON
WENT DOWN WITH H.M.S. GLOUCESTER

We discover Frederick Howard Thompson in the 1901 census, aged three, living at Hillside Terrace. He was the youngest of ten siblings, children of William and Elizabeth Thompson. William was a cadets' servant on H.M.S. *Britannia*. By 1911 they were living in a six-roomed house at Waterhead. Frederick, now 13, was a scholar at Kingswear School.

HMS Gloucester

We have no trace of him until we find his name on Kingswear War Memorial. Aged 42, he had become the husband of Lillian Thompson, and was an Engine Room Artificer 2nd Class on HMS *Gloucester*. *Gloucester* formed part of a naval force acting against German military transports to Crete. On 22nd May 1941, while in the Kithera Channel, north of Crete, she was attacked by German Stuka dive bombers and sank, having sustained at least four heavy bomb hits and three near-misses. Of the 807 men aboard at the time of her sinking, only 85 survived.

GERALD THOMPSON
SAVED A GIRL FROM DROWNING

The Paignton Western Gazette tells us that on 3rd July 1941 Gerald Thompson, a fourteen year old Kingswear boy, performed a gallant act on Friday afternoon when he jumped fully clothed from the passenger ferry to the rescue of Mavis Rowe, a twelve year old Kingswear girl, who had got in to difficulties while bathing at Collins Quay, Kingswear. He brought her safely ashore and first aid was given by Mr. R. J. Worth, ambulance officer, A.R.P., Kingswear. Miss Rowe was sufficiently recovered to be able to dress and returned home.

ANNA VIOLETTA THURSTAN
BRAVERY OF A NURSE

Anna Violetta Thurstan was born in Hastings in 1879. She lived at Dragon House, the converted Nethway School building, from 1935 to 1937. She seems to have re-named every house where she lived as Dragon House.
The Great War Forum on the Web tells us that Violetta Thurstan had an adventurous and varied career during the Great War. The daughter

of a doctor, she trained as a nurse at The London Hospital. At the outbreak of war she was appointed matron of a British ambulance unit to be stationed in Brussels. Hardly had she and her staff arrived before the Belgian Government decided to offer no resistance and the Germans occupied the city. Most of the staff were evacuated, but Violetta and two or three nurses remained in Brussels. Here she received an appeal to help the British wounded prisoners after the Battle of Mons. Almost single-handed she accosted the German commandant demanding urgently needed necessaries. For this service she later received the Mons star.

Returning to Brussels, he and her fellow nurses were carried off as prisoners to Germany but ultimately dumped in Copenhagen. There she at once volunteered for the Russian front, where the nursing arrangements had broken down. To reach the front she had to travel through Sweden. At that time the country was all on the German side, and she and one nurse, who offered to accompany her, were subject to many petty annoyances. Her first job in Russia was to take charge of a temporary hospital of 500 beds in the Polish town of Lodz. With poor food and only the help from two semi-trained assistants, she went through the siege of that place.

In the evacuation she narrowly escaped becoming a German prisoner for the second time. She was now advanced to supervise a length of railway, with a special ambulance train to carry the wounded back to the base hospital. She was dressing a wound when a shell burst nearby. A piece of shrapnel made a long gash in one leg. Septic poisoning set in, and for a time she was in grave danger and convalescence was slow. During this enforced idleness she wrote her first book, 'With Field Hospital and Flying Column,' which rapidly sold out.

This wound brought her the Royal Cross of St George, the highest honour a grateful government could bestow. Returning to England, her next task was to lecture for Lord Derby's appeal to men to enlist voluntarily and so avoid conscription. She was soon at the front again as matron of an improvised hospital of 1,200 beds, at La Panne, under the Belgian flag. This later brought her two more medals, this time from Belgium. At length, the British authorities decided to put women in the first line of receiving hospitals and Violetta was chosen as one of these. A farmhouse and its outbuildings formed the main wards while staff were housed in tents all round. One night the ambulances were away collecting wounded, under the cover of darkness and the staff were resting in readiness for the rush hours. In the farmhouse a priest stood on one side of a wounded man and an orderly on the other. It chanced that a German airman was cruising round. He dropped a bomb which killed the priest and wounded the orderly. The poor fellow was rushed to the first-aid tent outside. The airman saw the light and dropped his card to speed good work.

The whole of the structure was brought down and Viloletta was felled to the ground, concussed by the falling roof. She soon recovered enough to accompany a forlorn procession of stretcher bearers carrying wounded away, over a field of sugar beet in pouring rain, to the next line of ambulances. Violetta was suffering from delayed shock and remained more or less unconscious for three days. This won her the Military Medal. During this convalescence, she wrote a technical book teaching the differences between nursing in war and peace.

At last her restless energy drove her afield again. This time she had charge of a field hospital on the Salonika front. Here during a blizzard and a snowstorm, the whole hospital was practically blown to pieces. Before the storm had spent itself, she had boarded a goods train on the way to Salonika, where she drew all supplies and was restoring order in three or four days. A sharp attack of malaria fever drove her back to England for a long convalescence. On recovery she was appointed to the Air Force. When about to be demobbed, she was appointed to command some Arab refugee camps. Here she supervised Arab women carpet making. She learnt the skills from them, and became famous as a designer and maker of carpets in England.

The Paignton Western Guardian reported on the Spanish Civil War:
War News from Spain received this week states: Sir George Young Bt., the author who is leading University Ambulances Unit has arrived in Valencia. He is expected to leave shortly for Almeria. Miss Violetta Thurston, the Commandant of the "Unit" who did Red Cross work in Russia during the War has already arrived in Almeria to establish a first aid station there for refugees. The "University Unit" is the first British ambulance unit to go to the southern front. It has one ambulance and two motor cars. Miss Thurstan is a resident of Kingswear.

She returned to a home in Stoke Gabriel for a while, but worked through the Second World War as a Wren in a number of senior nursing positions. She died in 1978 in Cornwall.

RICHARD GILES TODD
KILLED DURING THE BATTLE OF JUTLAND

The 1901 census tells us that Richard Giles Todd was born in Exeter in 1895, the son of Samuel Whitfield Todd, of Boohay, Kingswear. He was living with his grandparents at 3 Hillside Terrace. His grandfather was Richard Bufton, aged 66, a naval pensioner. In 1911 he was living with his parents Samuel and Elizabeth Todd at 5 College View. They had married in 1894 and of their eight children seven were still living. Richard, aged 16 was a general labourer. On 31st May, 1916 the Commonwealth War Graves Commission tells us that Richard Giles Todd, Royal Navy, Stoker First Class, aged 21, on HMS *Indefatigable*, was killed in action at the Battle of Jutland.

Richard is remembered on the Kingswear memorial and also on the Plymouth Navy memorial on the Hoe. The loss of HMS *Indefatigable* is described under the section on Frederick Brewster.

WILLIAM JOHN TOLMAN
DIED OF HIS WOUNDS

William John Tolman is listed on the Kingswear War Memorial. We know that he was a sapper in the Royal Engineers, General Base depot.

He died of his wounds on 23rd November 1918 and is buried in St. Severe Cemetery Extension, Rouen, in Seine-Maritime. We cannot yet elucidate his connection with Kingswear.

ARTHUR WILTON TOMS
KILLED FIGHTING IN ITALY

Arthur Wilton Toms was born in 1924, son of Harold Albert and Ethel Priscilla Toms. He started at Kingswear School in 1929. In 1935 he left school due to "ill health". However Commonwealth War Graves Commission tells us that he was killed, aged 20, on 6th September 1944 while serving as a private in The Buffs, the Royal East Kent Regiment, and 1st Battalion. He had been fighting in the last big battle to throw the Nazis out of Italy and is buried in Coriano Ridge War Cemetery.

CYRIL STRATFORD TUKE
KILLED AT LOOS

Cyril Tuke was born on 23rd June 1889 in Kingswear and was baptised at Kingswear Parish Church on 8th July 1889. In the 1901 census he was a visitor in Ilfracombe and in 1911 he was a visitor at the catholic Presbytery Knaphill Woking. His occupation was Lieutenant in the Army. His regiment was the Black Watch (Royal Highlanders) 9th battalion; his Secondary Unit was the Machine Gun Corp (Infantry).

Black Watch uniform World War 1.

Captain Cyril Tuke was killed in action on 25th September 1915. He is commemorated on the Loos Memorial.

Cyril Stratford Tuke, of 16 Brunswick Terrace, Hove, Sussex, Captain 9th battalion Royal Highlanders who died at Loos, France, left effects worth £81-0s-7d.

CHARLES EARSHAM TURNER
LOST WHILE SWEEPING MINES

Charles Earsham Turner was born in Kingswear in July 1881 and baptised here in August of that year. He was the son of John Ellis and Mary Elizabeth Turner, originally from Norfolk. His father was a merchant and ship broker. In 1891 Charles is seen to be the fourth of nine siblings living with their parents and two servants at The Pines, Kingswear. In 1901 Charles was lodging at The Chestnuts with his now married older brother. They were manager and clerk in the coal trade, presumably working for their father. Charles married Mary Kathleen but we do not have details of his wedding.

In 1939 Charles is listed as living at Wing Tor in Kingswear. He is now aged 59 and is a lieutenant in the Royal Naval Volunteer Reserve. The Dartmouth History Group web-site tells us that he was a friend of Vernon MacAndrew, a wealthy retired ship owner who lived at Ravensbury House, Dartmouth. MacAndrew had a fine private motor yacht, *Campeador V*, which he had used to visit Scotland for the shooting every year. He used his property at Ravensbury and Warfleet to train unemployed boys to crew yachts and to be chauffeurs.

At the outbreak of the Second World War, Vernon MacAndrew offered *Campeador V* to the Admiralty for patrol work, and he volunteered with two other members of the Royal Dart Yacht Club as officers; one of these was Charles Turner. Despite being well over military age they were accepted as Sub-Lieutenants in the R.N.V.R. under Commander Davey, late of the Royal Navy. They were at sea through the winter of 1939-40, patrolling the channel against submarines and minelayers. The yacht was never designed for winter service, and the twenty two men must have been bitterly cold without the heating or ventilation systems necessary for it. On 3rd June 1940 she hit a mine off the Isle of Wight and sank, with the loss of MacAndrew and all but two of the ship's company.

TWENTY CIVILIAN WORKERS
KILLED AT NOSS SHIPYARD

On 18th September 1942 some German aircraft flew inland over Torbay and turned for a bombing run down the estuary of the Dart. The first of a stick of bombs hit a workshop at Philips' and Son works, Noss

Shipyard, where small ships were being built for the Royal Navy. Twenty civilian workers were killed.

Further bombs dropped in the estuary, sinking a floating crane, and a coal hulk. The last one landed on a garage in Church Hill.

A memorial was erected at the Noss Works, and when the Works closed the memorial was recovered by Tessa Gibson and transferred to Kingswear Church.

Here we list those that were killed with all that we have found of their personal details, some of which have come from the Commonwealth War Graves Commission. Presumably some folk were injured, but their names have not been recorded.

Frederick Clarence Adams, age 22, son of Mr. W. H. Adams, of 58 Victoria Road, Dartmouth. Husband of Kate Adams, of the same address. Buried at Brixham Urban District Cemetery.

John Richard Ash, age 21, Home Guard, son of Mrs. H. W. Ash, of 3 Middle Street, Brixham. Injured at Messrs. Philips and Sons Works. Died the same day at Dartmouth and Kingswear Hospital.

David Bott, age 28, son of George Bott, of Ranscombe Road, and of the late Elizabeth Arm Bott. Husband of Vera Bott, of 25 Crowther's Hill, Dartmouth.

John/Jack George Charles Bustin, aged 52, husband of Gladys Bustin, of 25 Hill Park Terrace, Paignton.

Rose Anne Crang, age 20. Injured at Noss Works; died the same day at Brixham Hospital. Daughter of William and Lily Crang, of 4 Greens Court, Higher Street, Brixham.

Thomas Farr, aged 58, of 3 Britannia Avenue, Dartmouth; son of the late John Farr.

Richard Franklin, aged 26, Air Raid Warden, of 183 Victoria Road, Dartmouth Son of Lieut. G. and Mrs. Franklin, of Eversrey, hitefield Road, New Milton, Hampshire. Husband of Jennie Franklin.

Lionel E. Holden, aged 44, husband of K. A. Holden, of 9 Ferndale Villas, Dartmouth.

Walton Lewis, aged 40, injured at Noss Works, died next day at Dartmouth and Kingswear Hospital. Son of John Lewis, of The Mount, Saron Row, Monmouthshire. Husband of Jeanette Lewis, of 182 Victoria Road, Dartmouth.

George Herbert Frank Little, usually known as Bert, aged 17, fireman, N.F.S. Son of Frank and Eleanor Little, of 1 Agra Villas, Lower Road, Kingswear, Buried at Kingswear cemetery. His name is also on Kingswear War Memorial.

Henry James Luckhurst, aged 70, husband of Edith Emily Luckhurst, 3 Above Town, Dartmouth, buried at Brixham Urban Cemetery.

John Martin, aged 48, hhusband of Edith Alice Martin, of Preston Villa, Milton Street, Brixham, buried at Brixham Urban Cemetery.

Sidney Pope, aged 17, Home Guard, son of Alfred William and Emily Selima Pope of 41 Britannia Avenue - Dartmouth.

Ernest Poole, aged 51, son of Mr and Mrs W. Poole, Brimscombe, Stroud, Gloucestershire. Wife of Edith S. F. Poole, 15 Browns Hill, Dartmouth.

Hubert Ernest William Putt, age 37, Home Guard, injured, and died the same day at Dartmouth and Kingswear Hospital. Son of Ernest and Florence Putt of 35 Sandquay Road, Dartmouth. Husband of Vera May Putt - 4 Grenville Close, Townstall. Buried in Dartmouth Cemetery.

Edward E. Trant, age 27, husband of May Trant, Yew Tree Cottage, Manor Street, Dittisham.

Nella Eileen Trebilcock, aged 28, daughter of Mr. and Mrs. Hugh Osborne. Wife of William Cyril Trebilcock (H.M. Forces) of Lanarth, Indian Queens, Fraddon, Cornwall.

Samuel James Veale, age 21, Home Guard, injured, died the same day at Dartmouth and Kingswear Hospital. Son of Mr. and Mrs. W. F. Veale - 1 Crowthers Hill, Dartmouth.

Frederick Vickery, age 28, son of Mrs. F. K. Vickery, 3 Curwoods Buildings, West Exe South, Tiverton. Husband of Brenda W. Vickery, 5 Belgravia Terrace, Fore Street, Kingswear. Buried at Brixham Municipal Cemetery.

Hazel J. Weaver, age 20, W.V.S., daughter of Frederick William and May Roper, of 153 Victoria Road, Dartmouth. Wife of Private Thomas Weaver, The Gloucestershire Regiment. Buried at Dartmouth Borough Cemetery.